C000291894

*Karen, Often fates le
value bette than o...

best wishes y...*

THE MAGIC IN THE SPACE BETWEEN

How a unique mentoring programme is transforming women's leadership

---

IAN WIGSTON
with HILARY WIGSTON

JOHN
CATT

First published 2021

by John Catt Educational Ltd,
15 Riduna Park, Station Road,
Melton, Woodbridge IP12 1QT

Tel: +44 (0) 1394 389850
Email: enquiries@johncatt.com
Website: www.johncatt.com

© **2021 Ian Wigston**

All rights reserved.

No part of this publication may be reproduced, stored
in a retrieval system, transmitted in any form or by
any means, electronic, mechanical, photocopying,
recording, or otherwise, without the prior permission
of the publishers.

Opinions expressed in this publication are those
of the contributors and are not necessarily those
of the publishers or the editors. We cannot accept
responsibility for any errors or omissions.

ISBN: 978 1 913622 52 7

Set and designed by John Catt Educational Limited

Endorsements

This is an excellent record of an inspirational and impactful programme that serves as a catalyst for future projects. The weaving of the practical and theoretical insights of the benefits of coaching, sitting alongside the actual examples, brings them to life brilliantly. A must-read for anyone interested in supporting women leaders to take their next steps.

Nicky Bright (Botterill), leadership development coach and founder of Bright Lead

Having been the beneficiary of mentoring myself, and as a practitioner on the mentoring programme, I know first-hand the benefits of collaborating with other sectors. Ian and Hilary Wigston expose us to an external perspective in leadership development, highlighting the organisational advantage gained through diversity of thought.

Colonel Lucy Giles, president of the Army Officer Selection Board

Thought-provoking and based on a wealth of personal experience. Great insights on raising our sights for professional development in the world of education.

David Laws, executive chairman of the Education Policy Institute and former schools minister (2012-15)

Contents

For Liz, Chris and Charlotte

Introduction

We are not what we know but what we are willing to learn

Mary Catherine Bateson

The beginning

Headington School in Oxford was founded in 1915 by a group of evangelical Christians, to provide "a sound education for girls to fit them for the demands and opportunities likely to arise after the war". Approaching the school on 10 May 2016, there was a wonderful aroma of freshly cut grass. Members of the premises team were busy making an already imposing entrance all the more attractive.

I (Ian) was there as a result of conversations with Charlotte Avery, headmistress of St Mary's School in Cambridge, who was the Girls' Schools Association president-elect for 2017. Charlotte had asked Bright Field, the consultancy founded by Hilary and me, to support her during her presidential year. She thought it would be helpful for us to understand the GSA's work by attending that autumn's conference, which was to be led by Caroline Jordan, headmistress of Headington and the GSA's 2016 president. So, ahead of the conference, I had travelled to Headington to meet Caroline. There was nothing to suggest that the meeting would be out of the ordinary.

The greater part of the conversation focused on the work of the GSA, with Caroline outlining her plans for the conference and me explaining the purpose of Bright Field and summarising some of our recent projects.

7

Then, just as the meeting was drawing to a close, Caroline remarked that one of the challenges facing GSA schools was the lack of women putting themselves forward for the most senior positions. "Men will see a job and reckon they will be good enough if they have six of the 10 key qualities needed for the post," Caroline said. "A woman having those same qualities will see herself as inadequate for the role and won't apply. I'm seeing it as one of the issues I want to try to explore during my presidential year."

I promised to reflect on this before the next meeting. Already an idea for a mentoring programme was taking shape in my head.

The following week, I had arranged to meet Dr Frances Ramsey, who was then headmistress of Queen's College, London. As well as leading one of London's most successful schools, Frances was chair of the GSA's professional development committee, responsible for the workshops and conferences arranged for GSA members.

When I explained what Caroline and I had discussed the previous week, Frances' reaction was very positive. The idea of a mentoring programme to support future women leaders of GSA schools aligned beautifully with the work of the PD committee and its goals. Could the programme potentially accommodate 50 mentees?

Some years earlier, I had been part of a team working with the Specialist Schools and Academies Trust, where I had helped to design and deliver a highly successful programme focused on community leadership. More than 350 senior leaders had taken part in the programme. Two particular features of that course had stuck with me.

The first was that it ran over 18 months – a necessary feature given the scope of what was covered in the programme. Courses contained within an academic year can come under pressure if illness or other work demands cause colleagues to miss sessions, but that risk is mitigated with longer programmes.

Second, colleagues on that course were required to undertake a project with their local community, aimed at improving community cohesion or furthering their school's relationship with a key local group. Building an outward-facing mentality in the minds of participants had been crucial to the success of the project. What if something similar could be achieved in our mentoring programme?

After the meeting with Frances, I got in touch with a number of my contacts in industry and the public sector to explore whether they would be willing to volunteer as mentors. Virtually everyone who was asked agreed to be involved. The list included Lt Col Lucy Giles, the first female college commander at Sandhurst, and John Cridland, former director-general of the Confederation of British Industry. It looked as if as many as 30 mentors would be available.

The next step was to get the GSA council to approve the plan. I met with Jane Carroll, the GSA's membership director, on 11 August. Council duly convened at the end of that month and endorsed the programme, with a proposed implementation date of September 2017.

A few weeks later, I had a meeting with Sharon Cromie, headteacher of Wycombe High School and the then co-president of the Association of State Girls' Schools. I mentioned my conversation with Caroline Jordan and asked whether state girls' schools faced a similar challenge. Sharon described an almost identical situation and expressed a keen interest in the fledgling mentoring scheme that I outlined.

The GSA's autumn conference was now two weeks away. Bright Field was due to sponsor one of the keynote sessions on women's leadership and Hilary and I discussed how we might be able to enrich the programme further, with the aim of delivering a soft launch at conference.

Little did we envisage that, three years on, nearly 100 women would have been mentored over three cohorts of the programme. From the first cohort alone, nearly 50% have achieved promotion. The success has drawn positive responses from headteachers, participants and the media, and led to our being invited to run a similar scheme in the US and Canada. The four-term programme now includes a variety of community projects, undertaken where possible in partnership between colleagues from each sector. These range from explorations of mental health and perfectionism to consideration of reading as an alternative to social media, and the development of podcasts for students at different transition stages. The programme has also included conferences held at the Royal Military Academy Sandhurst and Godolphin and Latymer School.

Why are we writing this book?

The seed for this book was planted in a conversation between me and Angelo Sommariva from the System Partnerships Unit at the Department for Education. Angelo's team is responsible for encouraging and developing partnerships between state and independent schools. He was so impressed by the model we had created in the programme that he encouraged us to document it.

As with the best coaching, the picture of what we wanted to write evolved. By the time we got to seriously putting pen to paper, Hilary and I been made aware that, worthy though this intention was, focusing only on the 60 women and their mentors from the first cohort would not really justify the effort others would have to make on our behalf to help the book see the light of day.

At this point, it occurred to us that the mentees in this programme were but the latest group of women Hilary and I had coached over more than 25 years. We've been fortunate enough to coach women from a variety of contexts: school leaders, an MP, early breakers of the glass ceiling who reached FTSE board level, and some of the most senior women in the Church of England.

The women we have coached all had differing views and levels of self-belief. Many (if not most) significantly underestimated their ability to gain promotion or appointments to posts at senior level in their chosen profession. In this book, we hope to offer something that may benefit women's aspirations and goals. By exploring how coaching and mentoring has supported women to overcome barriers and strengthen their self-belief, perhaps we can map out a helpful pathway for those following in their footsteps.

Many of our clients have engaged us to help them consider the challenges of moving from one organisation to another. This is something we have both experienced. For me, the decision to leave banking for independent consulting was made easier by the coaching I had received some years earlier. Hilary's decision to leave teaching after more than 30 years, to join me as a consultant and subsequently establish Bright Field, was triggered in part by a year of commuting between Suffolk and Bedfordshire to a job that was the most challenging of her career.

This broader perspective, then, seemed a richer seam to mine in terms of creating a book relevant to women and their varied leadership pathways. In these pages we will not only discuss the mentoring programme, but also the wider picture: the differences between mentoring and coaching; the use of psychometric instruments; and the benefits of having non-educationalists as mentors.

The writer and anthropologist Mary Catherine Bateson, daughter of the anthropologist Margaret Mead, explored the challenges faced by women in her 1991 book *Composing a Life*. Bateson examined the stop-start nature of women's lives, their multiple roles and adaptive responses, describing what she referred to as a creative process, an "improvisatory art". She wrote:

"In a stable society, composing a life is somewhat like throwing a pot or building a house in a traditional form: the materials are known, the hands move skilfully in tasks familiar from thousands of performances, the fit of the completed whole in the common life is understood. ... Today, the materials and skills from which a life is composed are no longer clear. It is no longer possible to follow the paths of previous generations. This is true for both men and women, but it is especially true for women, whose whole lives no longer need be dominated by the rhythms of procreation and the dependencies that these created, but who must live with the discontinuities of female biology and still must balance conflicting demands. ... Just as the design of a building or of a vase must be rethought when the scale is changed, so must the design of lives."

Finding our title and cover image

In choosing our title and cover image, we were supported by some dear friends and colleagues with world-class experience.

David and Susan Whitaker were coaches of the Great Britain men's and women's hockey teams that won gold and fourth place, respectively, at the 1988 and 1996 Olympics. David has been my coach in one form or another for almost 30 years, since he helped me to develop and implement a coaching model at Barclays.

The title phrase – "the magic in the space between" – originally came to David as a result of his interest in how players can best manipulate the space between them and their opponents, in order to give a particular move or tactic the maximum chance of success. It requires great understanding and awareness to make things happen "between" players.

In thinking about David and Sue's subsequent work as coaches in business and education, the meaning of "the magic in the space between" evolved. It came to describe what happens between a coach and coachee when genuine transformational change leads to a breakthrough in performance. This was illustrated most powerfully for me in one of my early coaching sessions with David all those years ago.

We had met at a hotel in Windsor. I was preparing to go to my boss with the idea of setting up what was to become one of the first innovation units in Europe. David's questions were giving me real clarity on what I needed to say and do, and by the end of our time together my plan was well formulated in my head. To my surprise, David then said, "I'm delighted you have such clarity, as I haven't understood what you've been saying for the last 20 minutes." I was dumbfounded on two levels: "First, how have you been able to ask such wonderful questions and give me such insight if that is the case? Second, what do I need to do to become more coherent?"

The answer to the first question lies in one of coaching's fundamental tenets, namely that the coach follows the coachee's energy, using their language and thinking to prompt each successive question. The coach draws out, rather than pushing in. The coach, paradoxically, does not need to be an expert on the subject. As for the second question, that became my next challenge.

The inspiration for our cover design also had its roots in sport. Dana Nunnelly and I were classmates in the 1960s when I lived just outside Seattle. She was on the school gymnastics team and also competed at state level. Since then, Dana's career path has included international marketing and branding, web user experience, graphic design, fine arts, and consulting. Here she describes her creative process and how she helped us to find the ideal cover image for this book.

"When I begin a project, I always ask the people I'm working with a lot of questions to help flesh out any visual imagery that they might have in their heads. They always have them, whether they are able to articulate them or not! I just help them get through that process. You [Ian] happened to be very good about developing visual imagery in our conversation and your sports [hockey] example was helpful. I first went to nature for the visuals, because sometimes something more abstract lends itself better to what you're trying to convey – it lets the audience step into the concept with their own interpretations.

"But there was something about suspension in air that I seemed to keep going back to. I've always been enamoured with silk aerial performances; it harkens me back to when I was a gymnast. There's a fabulous experience on the uneven parallel bars when you're flying from one bar to the next and you're completely suspended in air. The same thing happens in floor exercise and tumbling routines when you're doing aerials or flips, where nothing is touching the ground. There's something magical about the suspension that you feel physically, where there's space all around you and time slows down for a split second. It's about what happens to you in between when you leave the ground and when you land – it's a magic space.

"I was searching: what was it about that feeling when you're completely unhinged from everything? As I searched through different imagery, I found these two female aerial artists who were suspended in mid-air and then reaching for each other: bingo!"

Some months later, Dana told me she had discovered that the organisation behind the image was based in England. I got in touch with Rachel Furlong, founder and director of Tumbellina. She revealed the story behind the picture:

"You have to interest potential clients in different ways, just looking at the visual aesthetics of what the body can do. You're always thinking about the body in silhouette and what shape it can form. You want to try and get that angle exactly right so it makes a good image. Of course, you want very strong, very good energy. It's one thing to create the image, that's not enough – this person has to be giving out that energy, as if there's an audience watching. The energy is coming from all round the body. What's being conveyed is strength, agility, capability, what the body can do, precision, finesse. There's nothing left unplanned.

"Relating to the title [of the book], you've got two very capable women who are reaching towards each other, working in a joint capacity; you're concentrating on that motivation of future leaders, and you've got the gap in between the two silks. You've got these amazing ambitious characters, and you're looking here at the space in between."

Thank you, Hilary

Hilary's influence in this book and all Bright Field's achievements is all-pervading. When we originally debated the wisdom of embarking on the first iteration of the mentoring programme, which we did pro bono, she brought thoughtful and considered scepticism tempered with support for what she could see was a highly important project. As a coach and mentor to current and future school leaders, Hilary has distilled the wisdom of more than 30 years as a classroom practitioner and school leader. She has allied this with an innate care for people and an ability to hear the music and create the magic behind the client's words.

Both directly and indirectly, Hilary has contributed hugely to the writing of this book. It couldn't have been achieved without her knowledge, passion and judgement.

1. Mentoring, coaching and how they intersect

How do I know what I think until I see what I say?

EM Forster

In our practice, we frequently hear the words "coaching" and "mentoring" being used interchangeably. This sometimes occurs when clients are new to either process; they may have been exposed to a conversation where the objective was not clearly explained at the outset. Often the words are used in the same sentence, as in: "Our strategy is to develop a coaching and mentoring programme to strengthen our middle leadership capacity."

It's important to distinguish between the two terms in order to recognise the part each discipline plays in our work. So, let's define more precisely what we understand by "coaching" and by "mentoring", and how they differ from one another.

Mentoring has the longer history. Odysseus, when embarking on his journey to Troy, entrusted both his house and the education of his son, Telemachus, to his friend Mentor. The instruction he gave was: "Tell him all you know."

In our setting, a **mentor** will usually be somebody with expertise in a specific experience area, such as leadership or HR. After gaining an understanding of the client's needs, the mentor will endeavour to convey their knowledge to the client. This can be done in a variety of ways, such as imparting information, training or teaching in a directive manner, and sharing experience or solution-seeking in a less directive style.

A **coach** will frequently take a non-directive approach as they do not usually have subject expertise. Instead, their skill lies in asking effective questions and in high-order listening. They are capable of hearing not just the answers to those questions, but also the unspoken thoughts that lie behind the responses. Gaining clarity for the client and promoting greater self-understanding, possibly through creative thinking, are the hallmarks of a great coach.

As Trudy Hall, former head of Emma Willard School in Troy, New York, and now head of Abaarso School in Somaliland, observes: "The secret to good executive coaching is good questions. The secret to transformational executive coaching is the right questions. The best coach walks the journey with you like the best sort of hiking companion. At the end of the day you have gone further, had insight-filled conversations, and eagerly anticipate the next challenge on the horizon."

On occasion, the coach may be more directive (I take this approach only when requested to do so by the coachee). Even then, the degree of directiveness is in the gift of the coach. When a client is tackling assumptions or barriers, or their issue is low self-confidence or self-worth, there is a risk that they may latch on to "advice" and see it as *the* way forward, as opposed to one way among many others of their own creation.

There are times in a coaching conversation when the coachee will ask, "What would you do?" In that situation, I generally say I will offer my solution only when the coachee has given their response to the question. More often than not, their need for my view evaporates once they have thought through the issue. If they still want to know what I would do, I may make a point of stepping out of my coaching persona by pretending to remove my "coaching hat". Once I've offered my thoughts, I step back into the role by putting the "hat" back on.

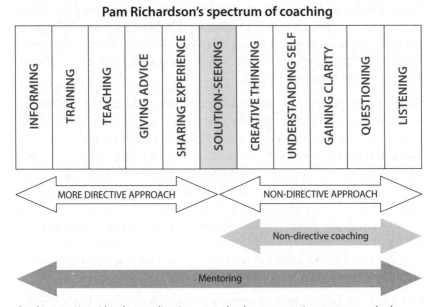

Coaching remains within the non-directive approach, whereas mentoring encompasses both directive and non-directive. Mentoring addresses knowledge/skills development. The non-directive aspect supports and enables clients to take responsibility. The client is always at the centre and in control.

Figure 1

Pam Richardson's coaching spectrum (Figure 1) helpfully shows the distinction between the two practices. In most of our coaching interactions, the elements used will vary over the course of the dialogue. We don't "turn on" coaching and "turn off" mentoring – the difference is rooted in the experience of the practitioner. Whereas teaching may lie at the heart of mentoring, the essence of coaching is in helping the client to learn and thus unlock their potential. The best mentoring will have a coaching mentality at its core: it is driven by the needs of the client, as opposed to a wholesale "showing off" of a superior skill set.

"Aha!" moments can happen in either setting. In a mentoring context, they could occur when the mentor highlights a solution to the client's problem. It may be sufficient for this to be pointed out, as in: "You can't expect to get promotion if your CV is vague and out of date." More often, there will be a shared solution-seeking conversation. One of our clients had entered into a pact with her partner. She would support his career, but at a certain point the focus would switch: her career would be given greater prominence, with support from him. This pact had not yet been fulfilled. What the client needed was a strategy she could use to assert her part of the bargain.

Coaching magic arises from a different route. One client's preferences – as revealed by her Insights Discovery profile, a psychometric we use in most of our coaching engagements (see chapter 10) – meant that she was often at least one step ahead of others. But this caused her some consternation: she couldn't understand why her colleagues didn't "get it" as quickly as she did – or at all. As a highly analytical and logical person, who also needed to engage with others through discussion and collaboration, she found herself having to manage her exasperation at others' inability to keep up or join up the dots. Her inclination was to step in and take over, rather than stepping back and supporting others to fulfil their role or complete a task.

Coaching helped the client to be more aware of how others might see her, and to understand that not everyone shared her quick thinking, clarity of purpose and drive. She also recognised that others often assumed that "I know more than I do". This meant there was an expectation that she would be the one to step up, and even an expectation that she would take on the larger share of the burden of responsibility. The coaching experience deepened her understanding of how the job was done well and she made those perceptions a reality. Her abilities were soon noticed and her path of promotion has since been steady.

"Aha!" moments can be prompted by well-framed questions that strike such a chord of awareness that the client is taken to a different plane of thinking. Too much subject expertise can get in the way of a good coach, who may unhelpfully impose their views or opinions. The best coaches do not seek to steer or direct their client's actions; instead, they use what they have seen, heard and felt during the coaching conversation in order to raise the client's ownership of the problem and, literally, their responsibility – their ability to respond.

As we will see later in the book, other sources can generate opportunities for transformational thinking – for example, personality profiling. The psychometric questionnaire we use, Insights Discovery, is based on the work of the psychologist Carl Jung. The wise use of such tools is so important in the space between the coach/mentor and the client.

As well as helping clients to see themselves objectively through a personality framework, and to understand where they sit in relation to colleagues, stakeholders and students, Insights Discovery often creates a moment of magic in its own right. Sometimes this occurs as a result of an insight into the difference between oneself and a key colleague. At other times, this is a personal "Aha!" moment – an insight into oneself that might have been impossible until now, owing to workplace pressures.

The most powerful insights are gained through self-awareness and personal responsibility. In that context, "discovery" occurs through the skilful and magical blend of the psychometric model and the coach's questioning.

Emotion in coaching

We are writing this chapter shortly after spending some time in a school where, in the previous term, two-fifths of the all-female leadership team had been diagnosed with breast cancer. Indeed, one was due to have a mastectomy the day after our meeting. This information was not shared with us before our coaching began. Both women chose to reveal the diagnosis during our sessions and, in one instance, during our first coaching conversation.

Situations of this kind are thankfully rare, certainly in the proportions cited here, but in our experience the coaching process frequently taps into deep and profound emotions. This should not take the coach by surprise: they must be prepared to respond appropriately, using their ability to empathise and allowing the conversation to flow in a direction helpful to the coachee.

Such a turn in the conversation may be more of a surprise for the coachee. "I can't believe I'm telling you this," says one. "How did we get on to this subject?" asks another. "I've not told my husband about this," says yet another, somewhat conspiratorially. Sometimes, a disclosure may occur as the coachee delves into previously unexplored thinking and decision-making processes. A well-aimed question, building on the foundation laid by earlier parts of the conversation, will often hit a raw nerve and open up a line of enquiry that gets to the heart of the matter. It may provide a healthy means of exploring a blockage, hitherto unrecognised, that stands in the way of the client's development and progress.

It's important to allow the client the time and space to explore their emotional response. Clients do not leave behind what's going on for them internally when they arrive in a work context, so it helps to understand how much their professional performance is being affected by personal issues. The coaching response needs to be non-judgemental, and the coach also needs to be objective and detached from the emotional aspects of the conversation. It is the coach's responsibility to keep the revelations, however emotional, rooted in what they mean for the coachee in the context of their professional role.

Accurate reflection and summary will acknowledge what's going on without escalating the feelings being expressed. Empathy, not sympathy, is required: "I can hear that this is making you upset" rather than "Oh, how horrible for you!" The coach must also remain focused on the coachee, making no reference to their own experiences. The coach's skill in working with the coachee's reality, holding up the mirror and parking their own stuff, is part of what makes the coaching conversation so powerful.

This is a good time to say that the coach needs to be absolutely vigilant and precise about the role and its boundaries. Coaching is not therapy. Unless the coach is also fully trained and qualified in psychological therapeutic practices, any deep delving into the coachee's emotional and psychological state can be harmful. Before the coaching begins, the client must be informed that the coach is not qualified to advise on certain aspects of their life or work. The coach must know where the boundaries are and be willing and able to say, "This is out of the coaching remit and beyond my capabilities. Have you considered talking to a registered counsellor/therapist?" By all means, help the coachee to acknowledge and name what's going on for them, but make it clear that the issue won't be explored further in the coaching sessions.

As a result of the Covid-19 pandemic, coaching is increasingly offered by phone or video call. The astute coach, having perhaps only the client's voice to go on, will need their radar turned up to the max in order to detect the vocal nuances that indicate an emotional reaction. Sometimes the client will let the coach know how they are feeling and they may even apologise, perhaps because they perceive emotional reactions to be unprofessional.

Carefully, cautiously and sensitively handled coaching conversations can develop the coachee's emotional intelligence, as they build on their self-awareness and self-knowledge. Coachees can give themselves permission to express/explore the more emotional side of things in an objective way. This may help to diminish the sense that it's somehow weak or unprofessional to acknowledge how they feel. In addition, the coachee's own ability to empathise with others will develop, enhancing their professional relationships and giving an insight into how others are affected by their words and actions within the professional arena. The coach's response and impact on the coachee can, over time, extend well beyond the coaching conversations. The coachee may carry with them aspects of the coaching practice that help them to reflect on their own work and behaviour, perhaps in the form of the coach's "voice in my head" or the "coach on my shoulder".

One of our corporate clients is an engineer by background who now runs the research and development function of a large UK company. When we first met, he had been invited to join the executive team as an associate member, but was struggling to settle into the norms and behaviours of the group. Part of this was down to differences in background: he was the only engineer in the team; the rest were either financiers or had a sales and marketing orientation.

Once our conversations got under way, it was clear there was a more profound difference. Our client used to get easily frustrated by what he saw as "posing" and inauthentic behaviour among many of the executive team. He also questioned why the CEO was apparently blind to their machinations.

One of our sessions took place immediately before a meeting of the executive team, which was to be followed by a dinner. Our client was keen to perform well in both settings. We spent some time exploring a paper he was due to present, with the aim of giving him as much confidence in his presentational style as he already possessed technically. At the end of the meeting he was beaming and there was a glint in his eye. "This feels like cheating," he said. "I can now go in there and feel as though I've got an extra person on my team, but all the words will come out of my mouth."

This was the first time I had heard the word "cheating" applied to a coaching conversation and for a moment I was stuck for a response. Then I shared a quote from the Gospel of Thomas that the management thinker Charles Handy had made me aware of more than 20 years earlier: "If you bring forth what is within you, what you bring forth will save you. If you do not bring forth what is within you, then what you do not bring forth will destroy you." This quote had resonated with me when I was on the cusp of leaving banking and going independent.

The next time we met, the client was itching to tell me about the dinner. "I got some great feedback from the CEO," he said. "I'd done the presentation earlier, which had gone well. The boss took me to one side as we were having drinks and said, 'You've got your mojo back!'"

If emotion is seen as "energy in motion", the coach needs to recognise that whatever energy is in the person is important in the here and now. This needs to be acknowledged and worked with, rather than against.

Location, location, location

In the early days of coaching, there was an assumption that the best coaching could only take place face to face. The commonly held view was that the coach needed to be able to see the client's location, environment and setting. They also needed to be able to gauge with surgical precision the moment-by-moment reactions to their questions, in order to judge, equally precisely, the right sequence of questions and observations to enable the client to achieve the result they were looking for.

In the introduction, I told the tale of a meeting I had many years ago with my coach, David Whitaker. David was helping me prepare to go to my boss with the idea of setting up one of the first innovation units in Europe. This was something I had been planning and researching for nearly five years (it was before the advent of the internet!) and I had arranged a dinner with my boss to discuss the proposal. Before the dinner, David and I could only find time for a phone call. But that call, which lasted nearly three hours, successfully challenged the assumption that coaching needs to take place face to face. For David, there was a sense of experiencing something new and magical. Already a great listener, he found that without the distraction of all the visual cues he would normally receive, his ability to discern responses to questions (or an unexpected or non-existent response) was heightened further.

The meeting with my boss was crucial to the next phase of my career. Before the call with David, my expectations of the meeting's likely success were low: around 30%. After speaking to David, I couldn't wait for the dinner. Not only had I built a stronger argument in my mind, but I also had a clearer view of how I could sell that argument to my boss. Like David, I had experienced a benefit in not having him across the table from me. Whereas I might have felt the need to be sociable and accommodating in a face-to-face meeting, here I was able to have my papers spread out across my desk, and from time to time get up and walk around to find a key book or reference to which David's thoughtful questions had steered me.

Before the dinner, I had anticipated that getting a result would take most of the evening. In the event, my boss said yes to my suggestion before the end of the starter. The challenge then was to remain sober and upright for the rest of the meal, when celebration was the order of the day.

Fast-forward to the present day and, as mentioned earlier, the vast majority of coaching conversations take place by phone, Skype, Zoom or other technology. The danger now is that a poor connection, inadequate bandwidth or poor sound quality (or a combination of the three) will impede the flow of the conversation and render the process frustrating for both parties.

What I want to explore in the rest of this section is the broader question of location. In our mentoring programme, we think it's key that the first meeting with the mentor should take place away from the school site – either at a neutral location or at the mentor's place of work. We are encouraging the mentees to become more outward-focused, so we remove the constraints of a school office, which can get in the way of their problem-solving. We are trying to take the mentees out of their comfort zone, so we get them out of the familiar setting of the school and enable them to spend time looking at themselves from a fresh perspective.

Latterly, the restrictions imposed by the Covid-19 pandemic have created opportunities for mentoring conversations in locations that might not have been considered previously. One mentee, Liz Cross, who teaches PE and careers, highlights the power of coaching walks. "For a person who naturally likes to be outside, having a meeting wandering around the Cambridge University Botanic Garden was ideal," she says. "I didn't feel like I was being questioned, but at the same time I felt like I was given every opportunity to really think about what it is that I want to achieve and guided to think in ways that that might be possible."

Once the relationship has been established, and once the goals for the programme have been agreed between the parties, it is then sometimes helpful to organise meetings back in school. The difference now is that the mentor can help the mentee see their environment with fresh eyes. And, in witnessing the mentee's working conditions, mentors are often able to point out helpful clues in the mentee's development.

Another factor that might determine the location of the meeting relates to the mentee's interests outside of their job. A client who is now a successful tech entrepreneur was having difficulties with her fellow directors. She was the only woman on the board and was also in the position of being a minority shareholder; their behaviour towards her was oppressive and verged on bullying. She was determined to find a solution for herself and the organisation.

As a former colleague, I had known her for some years, so I was aware of her interest in modern art. At the end of one of our calls, I asked her how much time she spent pursuing this interest, which brought a heartfelt response. "I'm a member of the Tate, but I'm thinking of cancelling my subscription as I've not been there in years," she said.

"What if we had our next meeting there?" I suggested.

"That's a great idea," she replied. "We could have our meeting, look round the exhibits and then have lunch – there's a lovely restaurant."

The tone of her voice had changed palpably in seconds.

A month later we met at the Tate Modern. Initially, she was unsure how productive the meeting would be, so we found a quiet corner and addressed one of the issues she had brought with her that morning. After quickly achieving one of her goals, we rewarded ourselves with a brief look around the gallery before tackling the main issue on her agenda. She acknowledged that the change in environment made it a lot easier for her to focus on the challenges she was facing. Her parting words: "Can we have all our meetings here?"

Since that experience, I've taken a similar approach with a number of other clients. More recently I discovered that a corporate client, who works in compliance, had an interest in photography – something we share as a hobby. We duly arranged to meet at an exhibition of the work of the photographer Don McCullin. With a tight schedule, we decided to have our conversation while walking around the exhibits.

We came to a photograph taken by McCullin in Berlin before the fall of the Wall. It was taken from West Berlin, looking over the wall to where East Berliners were gazing back with a mixture of apprehension and fascination. I could see that my client was drawn to this image and asked her to describe what she saw. "In my job, I have to take account of my internal customers, as how we behave and act towards them has a crucial bearing on how well they can perform," she said. "For me, this picture is a really helpful metaphor; although we work in the same organisation, there is frequently a barrier between our departments, given the regulatory role we have."

We have seen in this chapter that, even before the pandemic, mentoring and coaching can be used in a variety of settings. I am sometimes challenged by potential clients that coaching is a time-consuming process. Particularly in an education context, where professional development is often rationed into minuscule chunks, there can be a view that "we don't have time for that". But whenever we start a mentoring or coaching relationship, one of the things I say to a client is, "If you have an issue, don't feel you have to wait until our next meeting to raise it." Often a short call of no more than 10-15 minutes will help the client find the answer they are searching for – the result of a well-focused question or series of questions.

For most of our colleagues on the mentoring programme, this was their first experience of being mentored. We will hear in the next chapter some of their observations and reactions to the experience, as well as hearing from some of the mentors.

2. Reflections from mentees and mentors

After the conversation with Caroline Jordan that sparked the idea for the mentoring initiative, I began the job of recruiting mentors for what was initially to be an independent sector programme. A look at the geographic distribution of Girls' Schools Association schools revealed a preponderance in the south and west, but with a healthy array in the Midlands and the north. I wanted as far as possible to reflect that in the mentoring team (the proximity of mentors and mentees is less relevant now, post-Covid). When the Association of State Girls' Schools joined the programme, their locations were a close match.

We set the following simple criteria for mentors:

- They could be of either gender.
- They should have previous experience of mentoring.

Some of them were also coaches, but as the focus of the programme was mentoring, I was more concerned to recruit from a wide variety of functions. In the end, we signed up former CEOs or equivalent, HR directors, and generalists from the private, public and military sectors. We did not recruit any educationalists, lest the temptation to transfer education-based skills prevailed over the need to deliver leadership lessons (we were mentoring leadership, not headship, as this was catered for by other programmes run by the GSA and ASGS).

Initially, this decision was questioned by one or two of the mentees, but after the introductory meetings it became clear to them why we had taken this approach. The mentees also gained a broader perspective once they had partnered with a colleague from the other sector.

Some of the mentors were anxious about the preparation they would receive. It was agreed that they would get an information pack from the candidates, comprising their CV, Insights Discovery profile and two-part application form – one part completed by the mentee's headteacher (their sponsor) and the other by the mentee. There was no training for the mentors, because we didn't have the budget for it and their geographic distribution (from Dundee to Bristol, Lancashire to Surrey) meant that getting the mentors in one place would have been near impossible in those pre-Covid days.

In my briefing to the mentors, I stressed that I did not want them to adopt a prescriptive approach. There were 63 mentees, each of whom had very different needs and case histories. The key was to get to know the mentee and build a relationship that could deliver transformational change.

There were some early success stories. Suzanne Lewis-Dale had been apprehensive about being mentored by a nationally known figure, but she emailed me after her first meeting to say: "I cannot fully describe the positive impact meeting up with my mentor had. It was an incredibly self-indulgent thing to do, spending time to think and talk through your aspirations. We met three days before the start of term. I don't think that I recall ever going back to work with such enthusiasm and focus."

When I asked Suzanne more specifically what had been so powerful, she was very clear: "It was the opportunity to vocalise what was going on for me … I hadn't had that opportunity previously to actively reflect on my career and aspirations."

Before meeting her mentor, Richard Pelly, Helen Simpson had been sent his CV and confessed to feeling somewhat intimidated by his OBE. On meeting him, however, that sense dissipated and her subsequent experience proved very positive. As Rachael Warwick, a supporter of the programme and the 2019-20 president of the Association of School and College Leaders, says in the next chapter: "Pairing ambitious and nascent female school leaders with experienced counterparts from other sectors creates a wonderful dynamic. Professional mentorship is a powerful thing."

Amy Chapman was the first from the cohort to attain a headship. When we had spoken at the start of the programme, she'd seen herself as a couple of years away from her next move. A few months later, soon after her first mentoring session, she was shortlisted for the headship of Derby High School, where she'd previously been deputy head. She was successful and took up the post shortly thereafter. An economist by training, Amy was quick to see that Derby High would be more viable as a co-ed school. Almost her first decision, in conjunction with the governing body, was to pave the way for the admission of boys into Year 7 for the coming term.

Other mentees had equally positive experiences of the programme. Dr Charlotte Exon, director of music at Downe House in Berkshire, said: "Having a mentor has made such a difference to me. It's added impetus. For me, it's fantastic to have that external support that ironically has nothing to do with schools. It has made me more reflective, more outward-looking."

Simone Niblock was another of the initial cohort to gain a headship. "The mentoring programme was fundamental to my eventual appointment as a head," she said. "The quality of the mentoring and the efficacy of the feedback given provided me with a great deal of insight into my leadership style, personal strengths and interpersonal skills."

Hannah O'Rourke shared these words about the programme: "Being able to share that experience with my mentor, and talk through situations and scenarios and gain her insights, has been really useful in developing my own experience ... To see a woman in such a demanding and challenging role, and how she copes with that in terms of balancing her home life, has been really useful in developing my own confidence and leadership skills."

Some of the mentors found the experience eye-opening. Lucy Giles, then a Lieutenant Colonel and the first female college commander at Sandhurst, commented on the lack of training in the education sector in comparison with the Army: "There's a lack of training to prepare people for the additional responsibility of leadership. You're just landed in there and expected to get on with it – and, by the way, teach to the same standard you were doing beforehand."

Jenny Brown, then headmistress of St Alban's High School for Girls in Hertfordshire, and the sponsor of two mentees, said: "I absolutely loved the idea of a virtuous circle of mentors and mentees growing together. We have a massive amount to learn – we should be learning from the commercial world and business in the education system, so it was a perfect triangle."

Bex Tear, headmistress of Badminton School in Bristol, was an early supporter of the programme. "The journey through mentoring and collaborative working helped the mentees to think differently, get out of the silo of our school and their day-to-day role, and become bigger-picture thinkers," she said. "This has had longer-term gains in the colleagues involved: they feel confident in their place in the school and their ability to add value to the whole; they have the self-assurance to reach out beyond our school."

Q&A: John Cridland

Another mentor, John Cridland, had taken a particular interest in education during his 33 years at the Confederation of British Industry. The CBI's *First Steps: a new approach for our schools*, published in 2012, had been hailed as one of the most thoughtful papers on education since the publication of Ken Robinson's *All Our Futures: creativity, culture and education* some 13 years earlier. Here, John answers some questions that I put to him about the mentoring programme.

What was your previous experience of mentoring?

"I had been asked on a number of occasions to help develop senior executives in other organisations. I took those on selectively because I was a full-time executive and had limited free time, but if I could help I would. That interested me, in terms of transferable experience, in the following question: 'When one has had an experience, you've got fairly firm views about what you've learned – can you apply them in a different context?'

"What you as a mentor need to do is to adapt what you know to the fact that you know the situation is never going to quite be the same. You've had flared trousers in the attic for 40 years and think that it will be OK to wear them when they're next in fashion and realise it doesn't quite work like that!"

What had you learned about the education system from First Steps?

"As an individual, parent and citizen, I clearly had views about the school system and if I were to summarise those in a nutshell, I would say it's a system under great pressure – people being asked to do a lot of managerial intervention.

"[When we were writing *First Steps*] what concerned us was that teachers felt hugely under pressure. So, trying to help any of those individual teachers, there were lots of questions about whether teachers or junior leaders wanted to move into leadership roles, and whether a leadership role would take them away from their professional discipline or subject. It's a standard question if you're in a professional or technical career: do you wish to move away from that to become a leader? It's tempting in some ways, frustrating in others. But this was a more serious point: would my values be compromised if I took on a leadership role? A teacher might ask, 'In the context of multi-academy trusts with levels of management above me, would I become a cog in a managerial wheel and actually be asked to do things I wouldn't necessarily want to do?'"

What was your experience of the mentoring programme?

"I sensed that neither of my mentees had received a lot of help or preparation to take that next step and were, to an extent, scratching their heads asking all the right questions, but looking for guidance, support, advice, information about what they needed to do next.

"I felt I probably ended up helping them on a different question from the one I thought I would be helping them with. Clearly there was a question: did they want to make that step? Had they thought about what they would be letting go of as well as what they would be taking on? Would a leadership role actually be what they wanted to do? We did talk about that, that was important – helping them develop and polish a CV, of course – but I felt there was a deeper subject of discussion.

"I wouldn't go so far as to say building confidence, because that sounds flippant – it was more subtle than that. It was re-emphasising their satisfaction, what they were good at and what they had to offer. I felt that in both cases they tended to undervalue their achievements: they weren't looking to be told they were doing great things, but I felt the assurance I was able to offer, which I felt looking at each of their CVs, was that they had a lot to offer. That was actually a vital part of the process. It wasn't that they were unconfident – they had a lot to offer as professionals – but it was assuring them of their confidence, validating their confidence simply with a third-eye point of view, somebody not in the education system.

"We talked about pressure and especially the pressure that those in leadership positions are under. I wasn't surprised, but I was really struck by the amount of time we spent in the conversations talking about the conflict situations they had been dealing with. We spent a lot of time talking about how those individuals had dealt with difficult relations with peers, difficult issues with parents. Less so with students – the bread and butter of what they did, which was probably covered off in teacher training to a degree. One of the reasons why in both cases I did have the strong sense that they could move rapidly to more senior leadership roles, either in teaching or in the private sector, was that they illustrated how much of their time, in the positions they had been in, was spent dealing with difficult situations."

Q&A: Suzanne White

Mentor Suzanne White had been the HR director of Lighter Life. Now an independent coach, HR consultant and school governor, she brought a powerful external perspective to her mentoring.

How was mentoring in education different from other sectors?

"There were similarities and differences. The majority of mentees were quite unfamiliar with the process of mentoring or coaching within education: they arrived at the first sessions not knowing quite what to expect, as though they were attending an interview, so getting them to relax was quite important. Getting them to share their true vulnerabilities and the voice within their head, perhaps over cups of tea or cappuccinos.

"Wearing my school and my HR hat, a school is an organisation and so there are lots of common themes and challenges irrespective of the sector, in terms of setting vision, communicating that vision, and engaging your team to get there. There's a saying, 'Your vibe attracts your tribe', which is common to all leaders irrespective of sector.

"It's them understanding who they are as a leader, rather than the leader they 'should' be or 'ought' to be – enabling them to be comfortable in their own skin to be the leader they *want* to be.

"They might have some role models, and look at what skills they need to develop, but actually what was most important was giving them permission to be *them*, instead of asking 'What should I be?', 'What ought I to be, but I'm not?'

"If you've experienced good leadership yourself, or bad leadership, it's about: how do you want people to look up to you as a leader? What's the legacy you want to leave behind? That's quite freeing for many mentees – to realise that they're not having to try and be something else. There's no one type of leader that's the best type of leader. We need different work-style practices to adapt and be flexible with what we're having to deal with as a leader."

Did you find the mentees had role models inside education, or were their role models from other places?

"They tended to be within education – experiences they'd had from a headteacher. Some of those were quite powerful and sometimes they weren't positive experiences. [The mentees] tended to be in close proximity with whom they were working with; it could widen their perception if they looked at other people as well.

"It actually provides more innovation and freedom to have a box of the people they admire outside of education. They have more confidence when they can be themselves rather than try to be someone else. Perhaps learning strategies and learning qualities they admire, but if you're being yourself it's less stressful – you're not trying to put on a mask that at times you can't keep up."

Were there any particular highlights or case studies?

"I've done mentoring sessions in rooms where the mentee's lessons are going to be delivered, so we've mentally realised and rehearsed success in the same way an athlete does. Sometimes we've gone to locations where mentees have felt uncomfortable and they're going to have to perform, particularly where [one mentee] had a new role in a new school, and it was now time to prove herself and create productive working relationships within a team that had become stagnant in its way of working. She felt quite uncomfortable in its way of working. We went to where she was going to present and did some coaching work, so she could rehearse success in the environment where she was going to have to be successful. That was really positive.

"Because of Covid-19 we've had sessions over Zoom, been interrupted by dogs and cats. Equally, that's been interesting as you've got to know a little bit about them personally. You get to see their personal environment – they're more relaxed in their home scenario and that's allowed almost another level of individuals feeling relaxed and sharing. Because they're in a different space, they can take that mask off from the role and just be themselves. Sitting in a neutral place has been very useful and productive. I've had teachers where we've been in a neutral place and they've asked me to see them at their school; I've seen how they're interacting with colleagues and how sometimes that's been a good observation. We've also looked at difficult conversations and developing skills around handling conflict.

"Experiencing that process of taking time out, stopping and allowing them to observe, is like switching on that new brighter light of self-awareness, to do something different at the end of each session. That's been really powerful, as you don't often have the luxury to actually stop and take time out, and just breathe and watch and observe yourself.

"I did have one teacher, one of my new mentees, where the technology was so bad that I had to say, 'Is it OK if we just speak over audio?' I noticed that allowed that individual to be more relaxed, without that visual distraction, and open up her vulnerability to that deeper level.

"What's also been particularly valuable is the fact that often, going back, what's their first experience of their first organisation, which is their family. Roles within their family and the relationship with their role models, who are often their parents. They find it fascinating how, when we explore it, that plays out at a subconscious level.

"One teacher had failed an interview; she wanted to go for headship and was lacking confidence in applying for jobs, because of that fear of failure. So we explored what confidence would look like and what she would need, strategy-wise, in being confident about the process but also about the fear of failure. So we touched on that first organisation and it was really insightful – you could see her shaking with the insight at this new knowledge. She was an A* student and she got one B and her father just focused on the B. From there, we're focusing on what we can't do rather than what we're brilliant at. That insight, for her, was very powerful. We could then look at that situation from the perspective of her as an adult – what would she say if she had a child? We did some reframing and she got the next job, and became the headteacher of a well-renowned school."

Were there any particular challenges that mentees had to overcome?

"The key areas were confidence and self-belief to have the conversations they really wanted to have, if things were going wrong. Some of that was hard. For example, deputy heads who wanted to have conversations that actually they needed to have, but the headteacher wasn't dealing with it. Triangular challenge.

"Developing a growth mindset, which teachers advocate for students and sometimes they're saying, 'You haven't got it yet.' That key word 'yet'. They're wanting their students to develop that confidence and self-belief that they haven't got themselves. What would be the growth mindset for them? It's about making sure that they actually are taking action, that there's an action plan at the end, clarified and calibrated for them, and they're excited about doing it and leave the session with energy.

"That importance of calibration, both in a tone of voice and in its physicality, is really important to me. Sometimes my mentees are telling me they're going to do it, but I don't think they are. I will be quite challenging because I want to make sure that change is going to happen. That's what I'm there to help them to do. Also, it's about leadership – how they want to lead rather than what they should be. Because they think about what they 'should' be – the impostor syndrome – they hold themselves back. They don't feel they meet all the criteria in terms of applying for jobs. It's actually getting them to create a different mindset about what they've achieved so far. With one teacher, they looked back and realised they had got promotions really easily: 'I'm still young and I'm succeeding more quickly than other teachers; I'm young and now I've got this more senior role; I'm feeling a bit uncomfortable that I'm younger than some of the teachers I'm going to be leading.' She was learning to feel comfortable in her own skin because of her brilliance in getting there. That was powerful – looking at her success and saying, 'Why wouldn't it be like this now, because I've got that proven track record?'"

What have you learned from the experience?

"I enjoyed being part of the process and special relationships have formed, professionally and personally. What's clear is that the teaching profession overall is well equipped to manage change with students and parents. But they don't always have that training and guidance to manage peers and to have those important and difficult conversations, so that they can manage performance and navigate change and move the school forward. Elephants in the room are accepted rather than removed.

"It's been great to see that teachers do have a passion, they often just lack confidence and self-belief. Helping them achieve what they really want and make visible change in how they're developing as individuals is a privilege and really rewarding. You almost feel a bit maternal, because you're so invested in them to succeed and you've nothing but pride and joy when they've done the work to do it. I've had the privilege to be that facilitator, to be that sounding board, to create a safe place where they can be who they want to be, to say what's in their head. They trust you beyond the menteeship."

Melissa George, now deputy head at St Augustine's Priory in Ealing, was one of Suzanne's mentees. She says:

"From the moment I met Suzanne, I was put at ease by her warm, caring and professional approach. Through careful questioning, Suzanne allows me the space to reflect on my strengths and areas to be developed further, using her wealth of experience to offer sound, expert advice. After only three months of being involved in the mentoring programme, I applied for a promotion and got the job! I have gained lots of confidence from the programme and the support from Suzanne, which has enabled me to take the next steps to progress in my career pathway and reach for the highest levels of leadership in the future.

"Suzanne has been a highly effective coach. Because of the way that she prompts reflection and clear actions through her questioning, I have gained so much from our sessions.

"Using the Insights colour energies [see chapter 10] to shape our discussions, Suzanne has supported me to reflect on my own practice as a leader and coached me to establish strategies to move my skills forward. Our initial meeting was highly revealing of my strengths and areas for development and I walked out of the session feeling energised, with new strategies to put in place before we met again. Suzanne's coaching style nurtures confidence and self-belief and I feel genuinely uplifted and ready to make changes following the sessions."

Q&A: Caroline Hoare

Caroline Hoare, former director of people at the Girls' Day School Trust and CEO of the Independent Schools Inspectorate, is now a strategy consultant and mentor.

What did you contribute to your mentees?

"I brought a practical experience of a very wide range of issues both organisational and individual. I was able to draw on examples of different situations, as much as anything to help them to frame or reframe their questions or to distil a problem to make it easier to find some steps for a solution."

How did they react to you as a mentor?

"For one of my mentees, it was hard to get meetings set up as she was very busy. But when she did come to the meetings, she'd really thought about the questions she wanted to ask and she was quite specific in her ask of me, in terms, for example, of a particular scenario or how to prepare for a particularly difficult conversation. I think it was useful for her to have someone who was outside her immediate context, which was quite pressured, so that distance and making time for her was really valuable. She felt slightly challenged in fitting it in, making the time, and possibly slightly guilty about making the time for herself."

For those colleagues who have been mentored who haven't yet made headship, what might one be mentoring for?

"That's an interesting question. Even there, in the language, is that implicit assumption that headship is the be all and end all in an educational setting. It is the head who has the most impact, but perhaps it's about exploring how, within a school or at a system-wide level, one might be an effective leader and bring about change of standards or create a new culture without necessarily being the head. I'm interested in how you might constitute a programme that would help develop leadership skills in a non-hierarchical sense. In order to have the most impact, you do need to be in a senior role within the organisation. Is it also valuable to go through that process and realise perhaps that you don't want to be a head? It's expected of you, but you're good at your job, you're head of department, and maybe headship isn't the route for you."

What are your thoughts on what might be done in governance development to bring about a more gender-equal approach for selection?

"There's a huge step for governance training in this respect. Most people on governing bodies won't be teachers, and in recognising the breadth of the role of the head, you're not assessing their educational qualities, you're assessing their leadership qualities. Confidence in that area is sometimes lacking in a governing body, so there's a natural bias towards selecting the familiar, what might be perceived as a low-risk option. As much as anything, it's about being conscious in the composition of the panel and not just taking the people who shout loudest or the people who've been on the governing body the longest, but really consciously and deliberately trying to constitute an appointment panel that might not have the most obvious people on it, and making sure that you've got as much diversity as possible within that panel. However well intentioned people are, there is always a lot of evidence for unconscious bias. If you are an all-White, all-male panel interviewing a Black woman, she's not going to feel comfortable however well intentioned you are, so be aware of that and take some advice.

"If you really want to have a more inclusive and a more diverse body, you have to work at it. If you go to conferences and look around the room, there's awful lot of homogeneity and it's helpful to encourage a mindset that says that difference is useful – maybe drawing on work in board recruitment outside the education sector and recognising the value of different perspectives, avoiding groupthink. There are some big challenges there and not being afraid of difference is an important way of getting there."

When you've had coaches or mentors, what has been the biggest impact for you of that kind of relationship?

"I think having somebody who you feel is on your side outside your immediate environment is immensely valuable, and someone who's not afraid to ask you the difficult questions that you kind of know the answers to already, but you push down. Helping you surface some of those questions and not letting you get away with saying, 'I'll think about that later because that's too hard.' I found that really useful. Coaches who are interested and curious make you feel valued, more confident, and they can give you some very practical tools. We all know we have bad habits that we revert to in times of stress, but being able to recognise those and have a toolkit for ways of dealing with them is a really valuable part of coaching for me."

What have you gained from being a mentor?

"It's a huge privilege being a mentor or a coach. People have invested time in me, in my development, and I welcome the opportunity to be able to do that in return. You always learn something. It's a two-way process: it's not about handing down wisdom, it's about reflecting on your own practice."

3. Case studies: how mentoring makes a difference

Case study #1: recognising one's management ability and applying it in other contexts

Sharon Grant had a PhD and had been teaching chemistry, with varying other responsibilities, at the same school for more than 15 years. She was nominated for the mentoring programme by her headteacher, who described Sharon as "an excellent and dynamic teacher and head of department".

When considering the constraints on her development, Sharon, a single mother of twin boys, wrote: "Location due to family commitments and lack of confidence in management ability." This perception, common to many mentees, was not borne out by the evidence.

Sharon was concerned that working in a small girls' school for such a long time was likely to limit her ability to seek promotion elsewhere. When she saw her Insights profile, she remarked that she had once been much more dynamic than how she was described in the report. Addressing that perceived lack of dynamism was to feature strongly in the months ahead.

When Sharon was told that her mentor was a nationally known figure, recently retired from public service, there was apprehension in her voice. I reassured her, based on what I knew of him, that they would forge a very positive relationship, and pointed out that his private persona was different from his public one.

From the start of the programme in September until well into the spring, I heard little from Sharon besides occasional updates that the mentoring sessions were going well. She acknowledged that any feelings of intimidation had dissipated. She was making good progress with her community project, and had teamed up with a state school colleague to share contacts and organise a series of STEM visits/activities for students involving local companies.

Then, at the end of April, Sharon sent me an email:

> *"I am writing to inform you of my new job! After a lot of thinking and timing of events I applied for a job with Caterpillar as a Consultant Trainer/Senior Trainer. On Friday last week I found out that I have been successful and will start in July.*
>
> *"I hope that you are not too disappointed that it is not in education formally, that I have managed to secure a forward step??"*

The double question marks alerting me to some anxiety, I responded immediately to give her my congratulations and reassure her that there was no "right" answer on the mentoring programme. I was delighted she was going to make the move and keen to dispel any apprehension she might feel about stepping away from education.

We met for the first time later in the year, by which time she had been working at Caterpillar for eight weeks. She had experienced a very different September than had been the case for the previous 15 years.

"I'm surprised you and my mentor were interested in me," Sharon began. I replied that it often takes mentees a while to get used to having someone listen and pay attention to them. When you've been treated as part of the furniture in an organisation, it can feel strange to have someone's complete focus and interest for an hour or more at a time. I mentioned that a client once likened the process of being coached to luxuriating in a bath with their favourite candles and soaps.

Sharon said she was finding the language of the corporate world very different from that of education. When I told her I'd had a similar experience when first working in education after nearly 20 years in banking, there was a nod of recognition.

I asked how she came to get her new job. "I'd been working on my community STEM project and was due to meet Caterpillar to discuss arrangements for a visit that my students were going to make there later that term. Unfortunately, it snowed on the day I was due and the meeting had to be postponed. I was keen to rearrange the meeting and had to fight to get cover organised for me. Something inside me made me dig my heels in and argue that it was an important part of my mentoring programme."

When the meeting at Caterpillar took place some days later, it was with the learning and development manager. He was going to be the main point of contact for Sharon and her mentee partner's schools, and they spent some time talking about the plans for the STEM visit. Sharon was impressed by him and the work he was doing, and as the meeting concluded she jokingly said, "What you need is an assistant!" Unbeknown to her, that very job had been advertised on the company website the previous day. Another Caterpillar colleague suggested she had nothing to lose by applying.

Later that week she received an email from the company. As well as containing more detailed plans for the STEM visit, they were keen to know whether Sharon's throwaway comment had real substance behind it. This gave her pause to think and reflect. She'd been unsettled at school for some time and the more she thought about it, the less she looked forward to another 20 years in the same role.

Looking back on this experience, Sharon told me: "The mentoring programme for me was enlightening and life-changing. The programme made me feel valued, supported, worthy and listened to. At a time of huge self-doubt and confusion and frustration, it provided a forum for self-evaluation and spurred me on to make small positive changes that brought subsequently a huge positive momentum. I owe the programme so much and will be always indebted to how it helped change my life professionally, but also personally, as the changes have improved the quality of life with my children too."

Case study #2: enabling a more effective balance between professional development and family commitments

Gohar Khan's application to the mentoring programme was clear and to the point: "One-to-one mentoring will allow me to keep balancing my professional ambitions with my commitment to a young family." Hitherto her roles had been diverse across schools in Pakistan and Oxfordshire, but she was looking for "more experience and expertise" – there was a gap in middle management that she would like to fill.

Gohar's first degree had been from the University of Karachi, where she had gained a first in English, and her master's degree in Canada and PhD from Warwick University suggested someone whose career path was likely to be atypical. Her PhD had focused on postcolonial and diaspora literature about terrorism, with particular reference to 9/11.

At the outset of the programme, Gohar was head of ethos at Didcot Girls' School, a highly regarded state school in Oxfordshire. Her headteacher, Rachael Warwick, the 2019-20 president of the Association of School and College Leaders, described her as "aspirational, ambitious and clever". Rachael wrote that although Gohar was a strong communicator, "she would benefit from how she approaches whole-school change; she would also benefit from considering time management carefully, as she has a young family and a very busy developing career to balance".

Gohar's mentor was to be Colonel Amanda Hassell. Amanda had semi-retired from the Army and was keen to apply her mentoring skills in a new context. The partnership between Gohar and Amanda worked extremely well (and has continued informally beyond the duration of the programme). It would be wrong to claim that every pairing has worked as smoothly as this one.

More than a year later, in January 2019, I met Rachael and Gohar in Rachael's office. I was keen to make visits to as many of the participating schools as possible.

Gohar told me that, as part of her community project, she was organising a leadership conference to take place on International Women's Day, some two months hence. She had delivered a similar event the previous year and had attracted speakers as varied as her own mentor, Amanda Hassell, the scientist Baroness Susan Greenfield and Suzie de Rohan Willner, CEO of the fashion and lifestyle brand Toast.

The theme this year was creativity and innovation in leadership. Quite innocently, I asked Gohar how she would differentiate between the two concepts. Her reply suggested that she regarded them as one and the same. Prompted by Rachael, I explained that I had previously run Barclays' Innovation Unit, and I believed creativity and innovation were related but fundamentally different concepts. As the late Ken Robinson put it, "Creativity is the process of having original ideas that have value … Innovation is putting new ideas into practice." Before I knew where I was, I'd been signed up to speak at Gohar's conference.

By May 2019, Gohar had been promoted. Rachael, in her new role as executive headteacher of the Ridgeway Education Trust, had identified that the ethos role needed to extend across the full trust. Gohar had applied for the job – and got it.

Amanda's feedback was powerful on many levels. When reviewing her experience of the mentoring programme, Amanda said:

"I have found working with Gohar and attending your conferences particularly useful in gaining a deeper insight of how leadership can be introduced and taught to younger and particularly state school audiences, how it can be used to inspire young people to want to understand and develop the qualities of good leaders and to recognise them in others (teachers, public figures and successful businesswomen).

"I have always had to fight hard as a woman in a male-orientated environment, at university and in the Army, and I have learned much by seeing how things are/have changed – though there is still work to do. But I am hugely optimistic and inspired by the quality of the young people I have met through Gohar's school and elsewhere since being involved in this scheme, and witnessing the enthusiasm of the students taking part in the leadership conferences and in the work they prepared for the event. Particularly, I am impressed by how young women are embracing the opportunities now being opened up; they have few fears, really, and want to get out and grasp those opportunities.

"As an example, I can now understand why so many young women now say they want to join the Infantry (I regularly interview them as part of the selection process), when previously I couldn't understand why any woman would want to follow that career. It wasn't an option for me or my generation, and I feel I have been conditioned to dismiss it without realising the attraction for young women.

"In my role at Army Officer Selection Board – interviewing and assessing 16- to 17-year-olds who are considering a career in the Army after university and applying for a scholarship – I have to explore the leadership roles they have had at school or in clubs at a young age, and how they have accepted and dealt with responsibility. I have to make a judgement as to whether they would make good role models and ambassadors for the Army in the intervening years of sixth form and university before they might enter Royal Military Academy Sandhurst. My involvement in Gohar's leadership conferences has given me really useful context as to what can and is being done at schools. Particularly, the sessions presented by the students themselves have helped to contextualise what I often read on paper on a CV and helped to inform my supplementary questions.

"I have found Gohar to be a particularly enthusiastic and inspiring teacher, who I know will be changing the aspirations of her students and preparing them so well for making those important future life decisions. I am so delighted the school is creating a leadership role that will allow her to play to her strengths and capitalise on the fantastic work she has done in building the school's leadership and development agenda.

"It has also helped me to think about the presentation I am to give to my old school on speech day later this year, and I hope will enable me to pitch the speech appropriately to the young female audience, who will have similar aspirations and ambitions to Gohar's students. I hope to run it past Gohar before the event!"

For Rachael, there was a similar vindication of the programme:

"Gohar has moved from strength to strength since joining the mentoring programme in 2017. Her openness to new experiences and her seemingly irrepressible appetite for learning mean that she has made the most of every opportunity. I remember my challenge was for Gohar to ensure meticulous planning of whole-school events – she now has a Plan B, C and D for every eventuality! Twinned with Gohar's intuitive creativity, this makes for a powerful combination. I have also noticed how effectively Gohar has developed the skill of working through others. Following a recent and well-deserved promotion, Gohar is now associate senior leader and ethos leader across a trust of three schools and 2,500 students.

"Pairing ambitious and nascent female school leaders with experienced counterparts from other sectors creates a wonderful dynamic. Professional mentorship is a powerful thing. Gohar has benefited hugely from the conferences and the project work, as well as the mentoring provided by Bright Field."

Case study #3: internal and environmental 'comfort' holding back potential

Dr Davina Kirby was head of science at Ricards Lodge High School, a state school in Wimbledon, at the start of the programme. She had been at the same school for 13 years, since her NQT year. Reflecting on this, she says: "I guess being in the same school had somehow narrowed my ability to be verbally open and confident about my skill set. When you progress to the degree I had in a single place of work, you often rely on others filling in the blanks without realising.

"My sharp rise included being deputy head of the science department by the end of my second year of teaching, being an advanced skills teacher for the London Borough of Merton, an associate SLT member in charge of the NQT and PGCE programme and developing the school's behaviour for learning policy, head of biology for the sixth form, and a specialist leader in education.

"I completed an MA in science education, moved and renovated two houses, got married, and completed a PhD in education that I wrote while on maternity leave.

"'Superwoman' is what I often get referred to as, but returning to work as a mother, I felt I really had to prove I could still move on up. I returned, promoted now to head of science, but my whole-school responsibilities had been dispersed elsewhere, hence the reason I sought an external network to reignite my leadership skills once again.

"My mentor, Trish Dooley, knew my leadership profile and CV inside out, and she was acutely aware of decisions I would make if faced with particular questions, or problems at work in a leadership position. She made me aware of myself as a leader, but also an educator, and that I had skills, traits and abilities that any school would want. However, I had to become more astute at knowing how to compartmentalise these traits to then target these more directly to specific roles. For instance, a teaching and learning lead role would require me to put forward my understanding of teacher pedagogy and practice and student progress, whereas a role that would involve tracking students' progress would require me to demonstrate my skills at analysing data, and using data as a powerful tool for intervention. Both types of roles, however, would need to me to demonstrate consistent approaches, good communication skills, clear visions, and an assertive but approachable temperament.

"My first task was to read different job descriptions and see how much of the list I felt I could offer. Trish knew I would immediately sell myself short. I did. She reminded me of the fact that a woman can look at a job description and not apply for the role if they do not meet almost 100% of the criteria, whereas men will apply for a role if they meet at least 60% of a job description. This is called the 'confidence gap'. I was definitely suffering from this.

"As the programme progressed, I started to apply for jobs I would not have applied for previously. They were varied in position and sector, but I learned every step of the way. It may have come across to my current headteacher that I was not clear on my pathway, but by not narrowing my search I learned what I was suited for and what suited me. Then the real test: an internal position within my own school for an assistant headteacher was advertised, and I went for it. I was proud of how I did, but at the last hurdle I became so ill that I was unable to perform well during my interview. I really should have withdrawn, but I am also stubborn. I'm not a believer in signs, but it did seem like the universe was telling me I had to stop clinging on to my career comfort blanket.

"The process seeded doubt in my mind, that maybe I was chasing a dream I did not have the skills for. The 'impostor syndrome', they call it; another mental hurdle to overcome.

"However, it was during the February half-term 2019 that I received news I had been called in for interview at two different schools. I was still ill but I was also determined. I attended both. I succeeded in both. Around that time I had a conversation with Ian, who suggested that I should outline the criteria I was looking for in my next role. As a result, I was able to compare each possible role against my criteria. I decided upon the school that was embarking on an exciting new expansion. Although at first it seemed like a parallel move, what I had to offer resulted in my role being altered to be in charge of designing the new tracking system for the school. I will also be on the project development team for the expansion. It is not only strategic ideas that I will be implementing, but I will also be involved in designing and leading change. I am excited about the opportunity, especially as it has fuelled my ambitions once again.

"My story towards leadership thus far was about having a realistic belief in myself, and taking risks to explore other possibilities away from the comfort of the environment I knew so well. It is humbling when others can see and articulate your capabilities, but in tackling that confidence gap head-on, I can see continued potential in my own future."

Case study #4: recognising and believing in one's own value

Bridget Ward has been deputy head (operations) at Woldingham School in Surrey since September 2019. A former GB pentathlete, Bridget had previously been director of academic administration and director of sport at Queen's Gate School in London.

When Bridget received her Insights profile report, she was struck by its accuracy: "Initially I've always been very sceptical of these things, but it was 99% accurate. What I found most interesting was the description of my opposite type. When you're challenged in a job you always think it is about you, but sometimes you don't always understand what the other person is asking about you. I hadn't really contemplated communicating in very different ways depending on who the person is in front of you. When I saw that, it put me into context and it also put other people into context for me."

Bridget immediately began to apply what she had learned: "There was an opposite type who was a colleague. She was very imaginative, very bubbly, very outward. I was always trying to approach her in the way that I like. I'm very strategic, very logical, but I would almost send her off with an idea that she could run with rather than micromanage to get the result that I wanted. I understood that we need those people for me to be effective as a leader. But it was the timing of communication with her that was actually quite key.

"She would come in very excited and want to talk about lots of things, be excited about the day, and it clashed with my most busy time, trying to sort out cover and those sorts of things, so we would clash immediately from that perspective. So I would say, 'That's brilliant, but let's just pencil in a slot and then bring those ideas and we will discuss them.' It helped, as she felt she was being heard in a valid way rather than being dismissed. It literally changed the way I managed her. Weirdly, we've become good friends!"

There was a further, more personal aspect that Bridget's mentor helped her with: "I had applied to an internal job and I'd also looked at work internationally. I was kind of stuck – I didn't know where to go and had a lack of belief in whether I should be stepping up. By talking through what I was feeling and being quite honest, it actually taught me that I do have all the answers, I just was afraid to use them. My mentor, Suzanne White, was brilliant at that – we were talking through at such length that she would put it back on me: 'What would you want to see happen?' In the end, she gave me my voice back and also my confidence. I'm not lacking in confidence, but in my role I felt like I was at a dead end. I was resigning myself to saying, 'This is where I will work for the rest of my life,' and I was quite happy, but there was no passion to move forward. I was shown that I have all the tools to carry on in leadership."

Discussing the interviews that led to her appointment at Woldingham School, Bridget drew a parallel with her athlete's persona. "It was the calmest interview process I've ever had, almost so much that I didn't think I would get the job, because I didn't feel like I'd tried. I literally left here thinking, 'That was sweet to meet those people, but they're not going to want me because I was not nervous.' I had no element of stress around the day. I felt I'd been able to communicate myself honestly and openly. I got to that point of saying, 'If they don't want me, that's OK, as I'm not the right fit for them.'

"Previously, I had associated that being on edge with successful outcomes. Being an athlete, I had suffered a lot with stress and frustration and that kind of wanting to please others. If you put everything into something and they coached you for the last 10 years and then you fail miserably – if you don't succeed it is quite publicly shown. So that all transferred into, 'Why have I applied for another job? If I do fail it's going to be quite embarrassing; just another notch in my ability to prove that I am not capable.'

"As a result of the conversations with my mentor, I suddenly saw my value, which I hadn't for a very long time. Suzanne gave me the confidence. It wasn't necessarily about money, it was about setting the parameters that I was comfortable coming to the school. I'd never had that confidence.

"In my last two or three months at my old school, I allowed the team there to just be themselves and be uncomfortable with me speaking up and allowed them to see that I was authentic. I wasn't going to cause anyone any harm, but I did need to be heard. It really changed the dynamic just before I left. I think women have this a lot: if a woman speaks up they're being aggressive or difficult. I was in that culture where I started to believed that, which is quite strange in a girls' school.

"If I think about how my career has changed, it's such a complicated thing to unpick. I thought it was going to take two or three years to get somewhere else, but it felt like it happened on the flip of a coin, just by opening those conversations and dialogues."

4. Sandhurst conference, May 2018

The design of our programme deliberately went beyond the conventions of other similar mentoring schemes. The inclusion of community projects proved a powerful and valuable complement to the mentoring itself, as we shall see in Chapter 6.

But when we decided to hold a conference for mentors and mentees, we were following well-established precedents – for example, the work of the Mentoring Foundation with future women leaders in the corporate sector has been well documented. One difference was that we were working pro bono and without the benefit of a sponsor. Where might we realistically hold an event that would provide a real experience for the delegates, as well as the chance to meet and chat informally with their fellow mentees/mentors?

I had visited Sandhurst, in Berkshire, for the first time shortly after the mentoring project got under way. You might expect an institution as formidable as the Royal Military Academy Sandhurst, the British Army's training base for more than 200 years, to have a formidable entrance. You would be right. If arriving by car, you have to present yourself, suitably documented, at the gatehouse. The barrier is populated by two groups: Gurkha soldiers, friendly but armed, who patrol the exterior around the gates, and civilian personnel, who man the office. It all works with military precision…provided they are expecting you.

Once through the gate you are surrounded by idyllic parkland of more than 4,000 acres. As you drive through the trees to the main college itself, at a strictly observed 20mph, you pass buildings from different architectural eras as well as a large lake, which you suspect might be the venue for the occasional training exercise.

I was at Sandhurst to meet with Lt Col Lucy Giles, who at that time was the commander of Sandhurst's New College. We had met the previous year at another conference and she had agreed to be one of our mentors. In this meeting, it soon became apparent that Sandhurst was available as a venue for third-party use. We had found the venue for our conference for mentors and mentees, with the generous support of the Sandhurst Trust.

Our conference, with the theme of "leadership and identity", was to take place in Old College. Even by the architectural standards of many of the delegates' schools, it has an impressive portico entrance. On a sunny day in May 2018, it provided an inspiring backdrop for the more than 90 mentors, mentees and headteachers who arrived at the conference, from as far afield as Edinburgh and the West Country.

We had assembled a strong and varied trio of keynote speakers:

- **Helen Browning**, CEO of the Soil Association, also runs an organic farm and a pub in Wiltshire. She was mentoring two of our delegates. Helen is no ordinary farmer, having chaired DEFRA working parties on animal health and welfare, and at that time she was working closely with civil servants and ministers on the implications of Brexit for the farming community. She had also been a guest on BBC Radio 4's *Desert Island Discs*, which had highlighted challenges in her early career that we thought would prove interesting to our delegates.

- **David Laws**, a former Liberal Democrat MP, was our second speaker. I had worked with him some years earlier, at the investment bank Barclays de Zoete Wedd, and we had kept in touch. He was elected an MP in 2001 and was schools minister in the coalition government from 2012 to 2015. In my email to David inviting him to speak, I had written that his book *Coalition Diaries: 2012-2015* was "in many aspects the most alarming depiction of education policymaking that I have ever read". Those diaries are a stark and no-holds-barred account of the horse-trading that can go on when determining policy; I was keen for delegates to be aware of this, given the challenges heads face in making sense of policy initiatives passed down from the Department for Education.

- **Susan Ferrier**, global head of people for KPMG, was our third speaker. Through this role and her previous jobs at KPMG, Susan had acquired a positive reputation for her work in highlighting the need for gender equality and women's leadership. Based in Sydney but frequently in London, Susan's commitments had changed at short notice, so we had filmed an interview at her Canary Wharf office the previous week.

We had also asked two of our mental health colleagues, Steph McClean and Kim Hardie, to run a creative expressive workshop for the mentees. We recognised that this might be a challenging way of helping them to explore aspects of their leadership style, but all the headteachers we had spoken to before the conference had encouraged us to take their colleagues out of their comfort zones, in keeping with the thrust of the overall programme. Chapter 9 details the approach taken by Steph and Kim.

Insights from David Laws

After leaving politics in 2015, David had been hired to lead a thinktank, the Education Policy Institute (previously known as CentreForum). The EPI is a highly data-driven quantitative organisation that uses data sets, such as the National Pupil Database, to analyse policymaking and interventions. It seeks to improve the quality of education policy and outcomes through rigorous quantitative analysis, rather than hunch or ideology, which can inform the policymaking process in too many countries around the world.

David also chairs the Education Partnerships Group, the international arm of the Ark education charity. The EPG works in low-income countries, where the annual education budget per child may be as low as $40 or $50, to try to improve education outcomes. Sometimes there are lessons that these countries can learn from the developed world; sometimes they are doing things in education policy at a much earlier stage and arguably more rationally than countries such as England.

The EPG has found that, in the developing world, the demand for rigour and quantitative analysis is often far greater and more embedded within the education system than in the UK. "That is because, in this country, the expectation is that governments will decide whether to evaluate their own policies," said David in his keynote speech. "And there is a powerful incentive, often, not to do so, because government ministers and civil servants know that evaluations which are negative will attract a lot of media attention and reflect badly on the government. Whereas, in developing countries, it's often not the governments which have the budget to commission evaluations – it's usually the foundations that commission educational interventions who insist that those interventions are properly measured and analysed. Therefore, we have some things to learn from the developing country context, as well as our own, because often the evidence base around interventions is considerably stronger in some of the work we are doing in our own country.

"The desire to improve the education system has led, arguably, to a much greater degree of interference and micromanagement in day-to-day education than might be considered desirable. When I was preparing for this keynote, I was thinking of some of the policy decisions that I was asked to make during my time in the Department, sitting there with my red box that you get given as a minister at the end of the day.

"I list just a couple: I recall distinctly reading a 10-page submission one night to approve what turned out to be the transfer of two square metres of school playing field land to be used as a corridor connecting two parts of a school. That requires, in our education system today, the approval of a minister sitting in Westminster.

"I recall spending a long time with officials debating whether or not a teacher who had failed her pre-qualifying test in mathematics by one mark, and claimed that it was because the sun was in her eyes in the testing centre, should be given a fourth opportunity to pass, having failed three."

One of the themes I had observed with a range of headteacher clients over many years was the extent to which they allowed themselves to be swayed, often on a daily basis, by the stream of diktats that emerged from the Department for Education (or the Department for Education and Skills, or the Department for Children, Schools and Families, or whatever the education ministry was calling itself). I had asked David to address this point specifically in his speech.

"It's tempting, as a school leader, to be distracted by all these political things going on, but in my experience the best school leaders, while having a view on these matters, also understand that they have a massive amount within their own control and within their own influence that they can use as drivers to really change the things that are going on in their schools. The best headteachers that I've spoken to in the past are the ones who accept the constraints of the system and get on with it. And the ones, invariably, who go on longest about the mistakes the government are making are often not focused on the things that they could change themselves that are in their own hands. It's also true that many of the errors that politicians make in relation to the education system are not deliberate malicious blunders, but are a failure to understand many of the key and important drivers of policy. Where school leaders and the leadership of the education system can engage productively and constructively in the political system, there can be real progress and a real finding of solutions which work for school leaders and work for political leaders. It has to be said that the leaderships of ASCL, NAHT, and a number of the other education bodies, work very constructively on the whole with ministers and try to move policy in a more sensible direction.

"I saw an official recently from the DfE who I knew up to my time as a minister. He was moaning to me how difficult it was to get anything done in government: 'It's a nightmare. We've got so many regulations that need updating and so many things we should be legislating for. We can't get any of these things through parliament. We can't get any political time because of Brexit.' And there was silence for a few seconds and he said, 'Maybe this is a really good thing – we haven't got all this change and regulation and volatility going through the system.' And I think it is. I think it's an opportunity for what recent governments have referred to as the school-led system to start to influence and lead parts of the education debate, rather than waiting for all of that to be led, changed and sometimes distorted by Westminster.

"Autonomy and freedom to innovate and the empowerment of headteachers has led, in England over the last 25 years, to some very big successes. We can all think of individual highly inspiring headteachers who have gone into challenging schools, often in very disadvantaged communities, and set incredibly high aspirations, motivated staff (who will often largely be the same staff who were operating in schools previously that were doing very badly), and helped to turn those schools around. The sponsored academies programme that was established by the Blair government around 2001-2 was very controversial. But we have enough data now to know that, comparing similar schools with similar schools, whether they were successful or not, this policy has been a success – unusually for government policy interventions! On average, the average pupil in each of those 200 secondary schools changed into a sponsored academy has got one GCSE grade higher in each of five GCSE subjects, and the university attendance rate for those schools, compared with similar schools with similar levels of disadvantage, has gone up by about 40%. That is quite a large impact for an education intervention. Admittedly the university figures are not in the most elite universities, but it's still a very significant achievement against comparator schools.

"Are we doing enough, people are beginning to ask in addition, to get the best leaders into the toughest schools in the most challenging neighbourhoods where they can make the biggest impact? Many of the school systems around the world that are the best put a high degree of emphasis on getting leaders who are highly able to teach in some of the most challenging schools. Arguably, in our country, we have a bias in the other direction, and some of the accountability measures can dissuade highly able leaders, particularly early on in their careers, to take on schools in challenging areas. EPI published quite challenging data, jointly with Ofsted late in 2016, looking at the value-added statistics. Ofsted looked to be unduly harsh on high-performing schools with a high proportion of disadvantaged youngsters, and tended to over-mark outstanding schools with very affluent catchments where all the students were doing pretty well but they might be making pretty unimpressive progress.

"Do we really have a school-led system that politicians and others are talking about, or is this school-led system really outcrops of cooperation and excellence in a country where for the average school the sense of support, challenge and linkage really isn't there, and where some schools feel there is less support now for development, improvement and leadership than there used to be, when we at least had local authorities that could be consistently fallen back on, however varied their quality was.

"Do we really have a system of developing our leadership and teaching capacity in this country which is fit for purpose? Sir Michael Wilshaw, who wasn't always the most popular chief inspector with teachers and headteachers, rightly challenged towards the end of his time as chief inspector whether or not the system we have for leadership development is fit for purpose, and questioned: if we were running schools in the same way as a big company in the UK was running a business, would we have such a devolved and varied system of leadership education and training? Some of the sense that freedom and autonomy automatically improve conditions is now being challenged by both our experience in the UK and some of the international academics who are looking at this. Andreas Schleicher, one of the foremost commentators on education policy and data globally, has written that knowledge in the field of education is very sticky – it doesn't spread easily enough in countries such as England – and he's also pointed out that if autonomy can be combined with a culture of collaboration, not only will schools benefit but individual teachers will benefit too. He cites that looking at evidence from some of the highest performing systems in the world."

In conclusion, David returned to his earlier theme of the importance of evidence in education.

"It is very surprising that education is a learning, research-evidence-based subject instinctively, and yet if you compare the way in which we figure out what we should do in the education system to educate youngsters, compared to things like health, there is a much greater confidence in education in experimentation, variety, doing things in lots of different ways which are often seen as advantages in education, including by politicians, but which in health would be regarded as eccentric. If you went along to a hospital and were about to have a serious operation and the surgeon said, 'We've been innovating recently and have some great new ideas we're going to try out on you,' you'd think they were absolutely crazy and yet quite of lot of the schools reform recently (I suppose it was part of the Gove-ite philosophy) was to allow schools to decide what works best, allow them the freedom to innovate – they'll do a better job than politicians. Some of that might have been true, but it raises the more important question of: how do you figure out what works and spread it throughout the education system, rather than have people experimenting with things that don't work? I mean not just school leaders, but people in the DfE having a much greater commitment to the evidence.

"But I think there's a lot more that we can do in this area to help teachers to understand what works in teaching practice, so that they can spend their time innovating on the really interesting things that can motivate young people to engage in learning, rather than having to reinvent a different way of teaching and managing behaviour in tens of thousands of classrooms in 23,500 schools throughout the country.

"We've also got to do much more to train and develop our leadership capacity in England. It is startling that we still have such a randomised system of leadership development. I can understand why many politicians are nervous about creating a formal Sandhurst of Education: would it be captured by vested interests? Would it be subject to making mistakes and telling you one thing in one decade and changing it all in the next? Maybe the future should involve not one Sandhurst but a number of competing ones in the education sector, but I don't think we are going to solve our problems of leadership if we rely on 23,500 autonomous schools making up solutions themselves. And we've got much more to do to expand this professional development from the leadership of the sector to individual teachers. The world-leading countries are those who not only recruit people into the teaching profession but develop them over time so their skills and capabilities are improved. The international evidence from the OECD [Organisation for Economic Co-operation and Development] is the countries which most effectively develop their teacher workforce don't do so with a leadership style, either from government or school leaders, that imposes solutions on teachers, but manage to do so by engaging teachers in schools with learning, with sharing in best practice and making them feel a sense of ownership which arguably is not the case at the present time."

Q&A with David Laws

After David's speech, we opened up to questions from the conference delegates.

Madeleine Copin: "I'm a teacher of maths who's very passionate about data and evidence. Some of the things that are most important are very difficult to measure – for example, resilience, imagination, creativity. Can I invite your reflections as to what you would do about that in education?"

David: "It is a real problem if you're trying to improve an education system for which the basics aren't working for a large number of youngsters. Therefore, you have intensive focus and accountability on the schools to improve the proportion of young people achieving basic skills in English and maths. The risk is that you then start creating an incentive to not focus on other equally important things. That's toughest in the schools with the highest level of challenge and the lowest results, because they're the ones you're really forced to improve. Whereas if you're at the elite end of the state system or in the private system, and you're sure you're going to get great results, you can simply ignore all of those pressures and you can find the time to do all of those things which get driven out of the system.

"There are two ways of responding to this. One is to try to start measuring and holding schools to account for things which are not measured, but I think that way lies complete madness, because you end up having to say: it's not just these things which are important, but having a wellbeing class, X hours of sport a day, X amount of sex education per half-term, and suddenly everything you do becomes quantified and measured. The whole accountability system goes completely nuts.

"Once the education system has improved to the extent that averages in the tail have been moved up to a better level of attainment, we will get to the system where the intense hyperaccountability of today can be relaxed. I don't think that accountability and league tables are necessarily permanent features for our system and there are some good school systems around the world which don't have anything like that accountability and focus on data simply for school accountability purposes. I think that we need to be thinking over the next 20-30 years about whether we can move away from things like that. In the meantime, ironically, it's possible that one of the best hopes of pushing back against this data and accountability might be to use part of the accountability system that could be looking at things beyond data. In other words, at the breadth of the curriculum, at what subjects are being included. Ofsted and the new chief inspector [Amanda Spielman became chief inspector in 2017] are very concerned to look at things that go beyond data and accountability metrics, and comment on the way in which schools prioritise some of those other things which you said are important.

They will comment on where schools are wrongly directing pupils to qualifications which are there simply to get a better mark for progress, but they're narrowing the curriculum in the process.

"That's a promising potential development. The tricky thing that you have to solve before doing that is that you have to create some agreement in the education system, in Ofsted and preferably with the DfE, about what those other things are that are important. I remember having a very similar conversation about Michael Gove [education secretary from 2010 to 2014] and Michael Wilshaw having the most ding-dong battle between themselves about whether or not Ofsted should have this role about commenting on curriculum breadth and what schools are doing. Michael Gove was saying, 'Absolutely no way am I having Ofsted impose its idea about what the right curriculum is. I want schools to focus on three or four basic subjects if that's what they think is right.' Michael Wilshaw was saying, 'That's cheating – anyone can focus on three or four subjects and do well. I want great schools to do well across a range of subjects.' What you can't do to schools is send one bunch of inspectors with one view about what they're doing and another bunch of inspectors with a different view. I'll be interested to see if Amanda and Ofsted succeed over the next year in allowing Ofsted to have a clear but broader role and pick up some of these issues."

Michelle Malakouna: "I really appreciated it when you raised the question about whether we're doing enough to try and get the best teachers into challenging schools. You also mentioned the apprehension that teachers feel when they go into those schools. Are there any intentions from Amanda Spielman from Ofsted that there's real action going to be taken?"

David: "There are some small things going on. The Department has great sympathy with the view that headteachers in tougher schools have a tougher time in terms of accountability than people teaching in really average schools. The Department is trying to lean against it and there have been some small changes recently to try and give such schools more time. There are some national schemes, including the Talented Leaders programme, and that's an attempt to take headteachers from areas that are doing well and help them to relocate to areas that are challenging.

That's not an easy thing to do: people have family links, they have all sorts of other reasons why they may not want to move. We've got the first couple of cohorts but I wouldn't say that it's a national problem.

"Other countries have a much more sledgehammer approach. In the Far East, if you want to become a top headteacher and be recognised in your career, and if you want to earn a particular salary level, you have to in your career spend a period of time teaching in really tough schools. We don't have that system here where there is an expectation that people are in a national service, where someone in government can order you to move, and I think it would be quite difficult to introduce. We need to do more than we're doing at the moment, but we need to go with the grain with what people are willing to accept, rather than against, and I think things like trying to get Teach Firsters and others involved in education, who've already got that sense that they are coming in to help in disadvantaged schools, to commit not just for the first part of the journey, but getting them to think about working subsequently in challenging areas. I don't think we've cracked it yet."

Insights from Helen Browning

Below, you can read Helen's inspiring keynote speech in full.

"Ian's been keen for me to bring out something of my slightly unconventional past and some of the challenges that I've shared along the way, and I'd like this as early as possible to turn into a conversation, because I don't have any great wealth of knowledge to impart to you. What I'm interested in is having a conversation about some of the challenges that women face as we try to assume some sort of leadership, and our style of leadership and how it may be different from some of our male counterparts.

"I'm certainly not here for my skills as a mentor; part of my problem is that I think I always should be able to figure it out for myself. I guess that independent streak, that wariness that I have of received wisdom, can be a strength. I've also learned the power of a good question and the opportunity that sometimes being mentored allows you to stand back and take stock to have that moment of reflection, to think (which is the kind of question I ask myself all the time): what is it that I have the opportunity to do now, given my circumstances and given the skills that I have, small though they may be?

"I'm going to tell you a little bit about my own story, even though it does circle initially around farming, in many ways, coming into the world I came into. I come from a long line of farmers. I grew up and very early in my life I decided I wanted to farm. My father kind of patted me on the head and said, 'There, we'll find you a few acres and you can have a goat and a donkey.' But I was fairly determined, fairly early on, that I wanted to do the job properly – that this felt very much like a man's world.

"I was cross that I hadn't been born a boy, because they seemed to have all the fun and I was really attached to the countryside, the wildlife and farm animals. I liked farm animals a lot more than I liked people at that stage of my life. I've grown to like people a bit more, not as much as farm animals! I did want to show that it was possible for a woman to farm independently in her own right. I didn't want the life that my mother had, the dependency on a man that she had, so there was the bit of the young feminist in me, I guess.

"Nonetheless I grew up with all the aspirations of young farmers. You know that you must grow four tonnes an acre of wheat from your land, that you must get 10,000 litres out of every dairy cow – those are the kind of things you grow up with, knowing what you must do. It will show your proficiency if you can do these things, but I very much recognised some of the problems that were staring me in the face in the countryside in my teens. I could see the wildlife disappearing on our farms. I could see the way we were ripping out the hedges to make way for the bigger machines. I could see some of the problems that were starting to emerge socially in a village like ours. When I went to do my degree in agricultural technology, I was tacked to the intensive pig and poultry sector for the first time – state-of-the-art factories where we incarcerated pigs and chickens.

"It wasn't the kind of farming we had at home. We had livestock, but these were free-range livestock we still farmed in some kind of rotation. Even though we were by no means organic, we were very much at the cutting edge of the latest sprayer technology and that sort of thing.

"When I walked into those state-of-the-art hellholes, I was shocked to bits and it set up a bit of outrage in me, which is a jolly handy thing to have. I decided that one of the things I was going to do in life was that it was possible to keep farm animals in good, more natural circumstances and still make profits out of them, because if you can't show other farmers that you're making money then they're not going to do what you're doing or be in any way inspired by it.

"So I came back to the farm in 1986 to start thinking about organic farming, because that seemed to provide some of the solutions to some of the things that I was worried about: wildlife disappearing, animal welfare, our health and the health of the environment. Within three months of getting involved with the farm, my father said to me, 'Right, I'm going to leave you to it,' which was quite a shock.

"I was 24 and was suddenly thrown in the deep end with a whole bunch of staff – males twice my age – who were very sceptical about this young female who they heard had got these organic ideas that they were very nervous about. It was probably the most stressful time of my life. I used to have a complete breakdown every week. I would hide myself away, put a pillow over my head, scream and cry for an hour, and then get out there and pretend it was all all right. It wasn't, but we got through. I had lots of adventures along the way, but it was that baptism of fire. I'm not a natural extrovert.

"In many ways I had no great plans. My plan was to try and to do something a bit better; to try and do what I'm doing as well as I can today. Things have just come along on the back of that. I was lucky because I was a young woman in a male world at a time when people wanted to encourage more women into farming. I was doing something which was seen to be radically different, in going organic. We then started marketing from the farm gate, we bought shops, we did all sorts of things connecting with the consumer – something which farmers never did. So it did lead me into lots of opportunities to go so much further and have so many experiences that I never imagined I would have as a Wiltshire farmer.

"It's been an extraordinary opportunity and I guess I was really lucky in many ways, not only the opportunities I had but to find my cause early on. For me there is having something which gave my life real purpose, something I was trying to do. I'm a natural campaigner – in many ways that forced me out of my comfort zone. It made me do things I would never have done, including standing up and speaking to people like you. I was led or encouraged to do so by knowing that if I didn't speak out, if I didn't do things, that nothing would change. So in a way, for me, it was helpful because it allowed me to put my ego on the back burner. To say, 'This is important. I may make a fool of myself but I don't care, because this is how you've got to get these things done to move forward.'

"The other thing I found so difficult, and many women do find this difficult, is walking that line between confidence, enough confidence to make the impact you make, and arrogance, which just means you're a pain in the arse. It's so hard to get that balance right, and to try and make sure that every day you're in your skin and doing it from your core, rather than getting too caught up in your own hubris.

"For me, also, developing resilience. How you can keep going when you're so aware of your many failings. I have a kind of two-day rule. You go to bed at night saying, 'Why did I say that today? I got that so wrong,' and I find myself beating myself up in the shower. My rule is I never beat myself up for more than two days and every time I play squash, which is my great release in life, I say, 'That's my slate wiped clean' and I start again here. These little techniques allow us to keep moving on, allow us to keep feeling OK about ourselves despite all the mistakes we keep making.

"So I think that, for me, trying to keep some perspective in these complicated times, trying to keep some sense of humour about myself and some compassion about myself – we are all very mortal.

"This stuff is hard. I always think about politicians – it's so hard to get this stuff right. No answers in life are completely straightforward and I think understanding that complexity and that ambiguity, and still finding the route through it and taking people with you, despite the fact that there aren't any pat answers that you can offer, is hugely important. I'm also very aware that we women try too hard. The focus and effort that women put in is so commendable, but I know that my best thinking is sometimes when I'm completely relaxed, when I've had a run or daydreaming looking out of the window on a train, letting the mind wander a bit. It's too easy to lose the big picture by being too focused in all the time. Focus is important, but that ability to pull up is so important as well.

"I think we need to be nice to ourselves, and give ourselves that time to stand back and see the big picture, to try and work out what really matters.

"I have a terrible habit of taking on far too much. I'm running the Soil Association, which is a charity of 250 people, people working all over the country. Lots of really important stuff to do, particularly in light of the food and farming policy and the changes that are coming at us because of Brexit, so that feels like a really high-pressure job at the moment. The farm is complex: as well as the pigs we have dairy cows and arable crops. I've become obsessed with trees, with productive trees, with agroforestry. We have sheep, we're about to install another new dairy, I've got my daughter coming into the business as well.

"So that's a really interesting moment of change. We're very involved in marketing. We sell our products into the supermarkets, we have a pub with rooms, a restaurant in Swindon and I'm also trying to write a book. So, juggling balls and trying to feel calm while you're managing all these things. I feel as though, in many ways, the skill one needs is finding brilliant people to pick up the load from you, and that's what I most enjoy: finding and motivating brilliant people, because there are so many fantastic people out there, and helping to create the teams that have the skills you don't have, making sure you're building a team that does really complement your own skill set. That ability to hover, that ability to keep pulling up and to say, 'Where am I needed right now? That's going fine, that's going fine, bit of a problem over here' – that kind of ability to spot where the problems are emerging.

"It's so important to keep well and to invest in your own health and wellbeing. When you're on form you can do brilliant things in an hour; when you're not on form everything is a struggle. So invest in your own wellbeing and work out what works for you.

"When I'm looking for people, I look for the competence which you have to have, but after that it's all about the fit. Are they going to enjoy working with me or my team? Are we going to enjoy working with them, because fit is often an attitude and more important than almost anything else. Understanding your talent, understanding the people you're working with and what they need to be able to work well. What I try and do is often I just try and create the space for them to be brilliant. They're often much better than I am at whatever they do; I'm trying to take the crap away from them so that they can focus on what they do and be safe enough to experiment or bring their own passions to the mix. I always want to know what's turning somebody on, because if I can work with the grain of their enthusiasms we get so much more done.

"Sometimes, at the Soil Association, somebody will have a great enthusiasm, a great idea for something, and I can work with that. If one of my top people really had a bug about making sure that innovation was farmer-led, was user-led, and he developed a programme, he got the funding for it – you can work with that kind of thing. What I also try and do is the convening bit: making the team work together, bringing them together, trying to find a safe space for that team to enjoy working with each other and allow enough deviation, allow enough space for everything not to be entirely agenda-driven the whole time. Because sometimes the most brilliant ideas, or the breakthroughs, come when no one thinks they've got time to participate. That allows some of the new stuff or some of the difficult stuff to get talked about.

"There are always stones that nobody wants to turn over. And I think sometimes you have to create a safe space where those stones can be turned over, when they're ready to be turned over, and then you cement the learnings or the progress that you've made by turning those over and you can move on."

Q&A with Helen Browning

Gohar Khan: "If you had a room of girls in front of you now, what would be your key messages for them?"

Helen: "One of the things I would always try and encourage is that self-awareness and self-knowledge. Being comfortable with who you are and being clear-sighted about your strengths and weaknesses is a really big step forward. If you can assess your talents objectively and your weaknesses objectively, not beat yourself up about it and build on your strengths. I think we spend a lot of time trying to rectify our weaknesses and maybe it's better to concentrate on building your strengths – find the talent in yourself or in other people and work with that. To teach the skill of coming back into your skin is the other thing. If you're in a good place, it's amazing how you know how to react in certain situations and it's your subconscious in many ways. We all get very cerebral, [but I'm talking about] teaching people to use their subconscious as well as their conscious mind. I'm a great believer in sleeping on stuff, because your brain works stuff out. Ask yourself a question, go and take a walk or a bath or whatever you do – often the answers will become clear, your brain will work these things through.

"My own leadership style is one I have evolved and it's different in different circumstances. Sometimes I lead through doing, sometimes I lead through trying to inspire – you lead in lots of different ways. Sometimes I lead by trying to give everybody else a space to get on and do their jobs really well."

Natasha Dangerfield: Would you prefer 1,400 girls to have lessons in leadership, or for those girls to learn the lessons in life, in a similar way to your own experience?

Helen: "I've always had this impostor syndrome because I've never had the training. It's taken me a long time to feel as confident as I might have done 20 years ago. Having had a little more formal training might have made me feel less like I'm just winging it here, but there is part of me which enjoys that self-discovery, and finding things out for yourself is what life is about to some extent. I would always want to make room for people to invent things in their own way and to make them authentically theirs. I don't think we should be saying: these are the things, this is the way. I am really wary of received wisdom in that way. I want to help people think; I don't necessarily always want to tell them what the answers are. I want to provoke people, and particularly young people, to be thinking about it for themselves – that independence of thought, because we're not a flock of sheep. To use a farming analogy, we're more like pigs, with a curious, inventive mind, and we need to encourage that in people."

Insights from Susan Ferrier

As mentioned earlier, Susan was unable to attend the Sandhurst conference in person, but she and I had filmed an interview the previous week in which we discussed her leadership experiences and issues such as gender equality.

What, for you, are the challenges and advantages of being a female leader?

"Challenges involve several things. Firstly, I think sometimes the bar is held higher for women than it is for men, particularly female leaders who occupy very senior positions. The scrutiny that they face and the way in which they conduct themselves is at a higher level than sometimes their male peers. Men can sometimes get away with things. In particular, men can get away with a throwaway remark when they're in certain roles and that I think is unfair. Second, I think the challenges are that if you're a working mother, there are a lot of perceptions and unfair judgements that get labelled or used with working mothers, and that's hard to manage. Thirdly, I think that if women demonstrate emotion in the workplace, it can get very quickly labelled around an unfair sense that they're not in charge of what they're up to or they're not in control, they never plan, they're not focused. So that's the challenges side.

"The benefits or the value that I think women bring is that women bring people together in a way different from men. My generation of women, compared to my generation of men, we're more naturally inclusive, so we can bring people together in a way which looks for a collaborative, inclusive outcome. In many cases, women of my generation are less oriented around power; we just want to get the right solution so we bring people together in a different way. The second thing that women can bring is that we sometimes have different experiences that have incredible value, particularly in a world that is as disruptive, uncertain and volatile as we are right now. We've been less oriented around a vertical, simplistic pathway; we've had to dodge and weave and move in lattice career paths, which kind of helps with a different kind of decision-making which the current context calls for. Lastly, I think the human side of women – they're more likely to bring a human-centred orientation to the decisions and the discussions, and that I think is a real power that I often encourage my female leaders to bring to the table."

What sort of things do you do to keep your work interesting?

"I'm voraciously curious, which can sometimes drive my colleagues crazy and my team crazy. Ask lots of questions, read a lot, go to unexpected places, be close to customers, listen a lot, say not a lot sometimes, quell the need to be able to expound or make statements. That, for me, keeps things interesting, because you can learn a lot from others, learn a lot from context, be in the world, see things, take in external stimuli, which helps maintain a level of energy in what you're doing."

What are the qualities that you think are going to make a great headteacher in the next 10-15 years?

"One of the things I've been saying to my team, not just globally but when I was leading the team in Australia, is that we all need to become technologists in some shape or form. What I mean by that is not necessarily knowing how to code (I do think you need to understand the process of coding) but feeling really comfortable around technology. So one of the things I encourage my team to do is to download a new app every month and just play with it. Even if you don't end up keeping it on your iPhone or iPad or other Android, at least be investigating the world of technology on an amateur basis. I'd be encouraging headteachers to be really curious around technology. In my experience, headteachers are often a step ahead because they've often been using technology in really new and interesting ways. My children are being taught about robotics from the age of 6 or 7 in Australia, whereas I'm surrounded by colleagues who don't know the first thing about robotics. So keep really curious around AI, cognitive machine learning and the possibilities that that presents. You need to put it on a very positive footing – this is not about jobs being stolen, this is about new jobs and working alongside machines as trusted partners that can help the world be better.

"Second thing I would say is that the demands of leaders, including headteachers, are increasing, so keep investing in your own development as a leader. Keep going to conferences, keep doing this kind of work, because leadership for me is a practice, a bit like yoga. You have to practise it every day, so that means investment, that means making mistakes, that means expanding and extending your leadership capability, and do that for yourself as an individual but also for your team. So invest in the team around you and spend time doing leadership practice."

I'm sure in your role you've seen dumb things that people do. Do you have any advice on what traps to avoid?

"I can think of a long list which I've done, maybe I'll share those. Number one dumb thing is don't try and be an expert on everything. Perhaps don't try and be an expert on anything these days – be open to not having to demonstrate your technical excellence in every single interaction. I know in the past where I've felt the need to be the technical expert, you soon find out that others know more than you do, so maybe manage that for yourself. Second thing I'd say is trying to be completely masterful in your leadership style is pretty dumb, I think. You need to have a heavy dose of vulnerability and humility and be open to sharing that with others. I know in the past, when I've tried to be uber-capable and confident and on top of my brief, that you can soon hit a wall, so try and maintain a healthy dose of vulnerability. The third dumb thing would be when you do something dumb, to fess up fast, say sorry and really say, 'I'm really sorry' and don't make an apology which is like 'I'm sorry but...', then give all the caveats for why I'm truly not. Just come out with it and say, 'I'm really sorry, that was not the best way to do things.' Own your own mistakes and move forward."

One of the big things that you've been an advocate for in KPMG is gender equality. Can you say how that came about and how you see it as being relevant to schools?

"Gender equality for me is something which has been hardwired in me from an early age. I have an inkling as to where that comes from. It mostly comes from [the fact that] I've had some extremely strong women in my family and I've carried that through my whole life, so whenever I've had the opportunity and the platform to speak to gender equity or galvanise resources from an organisation to support the development or enhancement of women, I've jumped at the chance. So all through my time working in London I worked for investment banks where there were significant gender issues cropping up, so I was able to work with senior leaders to help them prepare a plan and prepare strategies for how to address some of those issues. It's been something which is very much a hallmark of my career."

What are the two or three things that you do to keep you in good stead?

"I meditate, I do yoga. I've only just been meditating in the last three or four years; I have my phone that I often use, so I often do mini-meditations. So on the way to this interview today, even in the lift when I was coming down, I did a quick meditation. I've got a real practice around that now, a habit I've built in the last four or five years. I'm very good about what I eat, trying to stay healthy in a new, demanding job. I've got a family which is very conscious of what we eat, so there's a lot of healthy food. I've got an amazing family which I draw on for strength a lot. My husband and children are my greatest advocates and champions, but they also keep me down to earth. I've got four teenagers, so they very much can switch between 'Yay Mum' and 'Whatever' if I'm getting too big for my boots – they bring me down to earth pretty quickly. I've got some really fantastic friendships that I take time to nurture and keep that group very much close."

What questions are you asked by women when you appear at conferences?

"I often get asked: how do you do it with four children? What I say when they say that is that it's really difficult for one woman's version to apply to other women. So my first response is: everybody does it differently, so there's no one cookie-cutter way to manage. The way that I manage is that my husband's a stay-at-home dad and he's been that for the last 16 years. That was a choice that we made and it was a bit of a pioneering choice to make 16 years ago. We both had careers at the time and that's been a really fantastic thing for us as a family, but that might not work for everyone. My mum is nearby, so when the need is there we ship her in pretty quickly. I use social media a lot with my kids, so I'm in contact with them daily. That has been a huge help, for me to stay in touch with my family, particularly when I'm travelling."

5. Community projects

Perfectionism is one of the great pillars of patriarchy

Toko-pa Turner

In the early days of designing the mentoring programme, once we had decided to bring the mentees together for state-independent collaboration, we needed to consider how best to make the partnership work in terms of leadership development.

As I mentioned in the introduction, some years earlier I had been part of a design and delivery team for what was then known as the Specialist Schools and Academies Trust.[1] The SSAT was developing a programme for school leaders with responsibility for community cohesion and approached me to help design the scheme. At the time this was quite unusual: the motto of the SSAT was "by schools, for schools" and rarely did it engage external consultants on work such as this.

The programme was unusual in its length: 18 months from start to finish, which enabled participants to develop their thinking and approaches to community leadership, and to build and implement considered strategies. Another innovative element was the grouping of participants by region, so they did not have the pressure of working with potential competitor schools in the same town. Rather, there was usually at least 50 miles between the schools.

---

1. The current SSAT is a direct descendant of the former SSAT, but is now a company limited by guarantee.

Taking inspiration from this design, we decided that each of our mentee pairings would be responsible for developing a community project, the difference being that their schools would be in close proximity – often in the same town or locality. It would be up to each pair to decide on the project's focus and to work over almost two years to deliver it.

There were three aspects of the project that we wanted to reinforce:

1. **Cross-sector collaboration**. Most independent schools already have partnerships of one form or another with local state schools.[2] These range from the sharing of basic facilities, such as gyms or sports pitches, to more substantial collaboration in teaching specific subjects. We wanted the mentee projects to be the roots of a more substantial partnership between the schools.

2. **Alternative perspectives**. The partnership element was intended to encourage participants to put themselves in the shoes of colleagues in the other sector (with one or two exceptions, the mentees had worked exclusively in the sector they now occupied). Each participant would need to consider the delivery of the project from the perspective of their own school, as well as a very different school with a different demographic. This would allow them to think about issues that they might face as a headteacher in due course.

3. **No constraints**. Our intention was to give as much autonomy as possible to the participants, so the project definition was left up to each pair. We wanted the colleagues to meet one another early in the programme and come up with a project proposal to which each could contribute. The programme was scheduled to begin in September, with the design deadline set for Easter; the overall project did not have to be completed until Easter the following year.

Some colleagues were frustrated by this last aspect and wanted more detail. Could we provide examples of other projects? As it was a pilot programme and we were still in the early stages, this was nigh on impossible. How should the project be presented? That was very much up to the pairs to decide, depending on the nature of the activity being undertaken.

---

2. This is documented in the annual *Celebrating Partnerships* report by the Independent Schools Council: https://tinyurl.com/11hfhlvu

The mentee pairs were full of ideas right away. After initial meetings had taken place between the partners, we received an idea for an LGBT conference for students. Another pair wanted to look at the differences between schools in their approaches to mental health. The projects that the partners ultimately decided to pursue were hugely varied in theme, scope and scale, and they delivered fascinating results.

The rest of this chapter will focus on a couple of case-study projects. The first illustrates how teachers in two neighbouring schools discovered that their pedagogy was inadvertently making their students more inclined to perfectionism. In the second, three English teachers from Birmingham developed a powerful approach to encouraging their sixth-form students to read for pleasure rather than spend time on social media.

Case study #1: Investigating perceptions of perfection and strategies to develop resilience in girls' schools

In a pilot programme, there are always going to be challenges to the design. We had hoped there would be a reasonable balance of state and independent schools in each of the regions, but in the South West this was not the case. So, it was necessary to pair Badminton School in Bristol with the nearby Bruton School for Girls, both of which are independent. Each school had two participants.

The four mentees were keen to explore the issues of perfectionism and resilience in relation to their students and schools. At a conference for the mentoring programme at Godolphin and Latymer School in May 2019 (see chapter 6), the group presented their findings to the delegates.

Alice Wyatt (Bruton School for Girls) introduced the project. "The biggest thing we spend our time on at our schools is girls struggling if they perceive they've failed or their desire to get everything right, even if 'right' is something that doesn't exist. After some discussion, the title we settled on [for our project] was 'Investigating perceptions of perfection and strategies to develop resilience in girls' schools'.

"To begin with, we decided that we would survey the girls in both schools and also staff, because we had an inkling that there might be a mismatch there. We decided to split the work, with Bruton focusing on the girls in both schools, while Badminton looked at staff."

Claire Peach (Bruton) took up the story. "The first question posed to the girls was: 'What do you do when you think you haven't done well at school or are worried about your work?' There were great similarities with both schools. 'Stress' was the word which appeared most in the Badminton responses, and was the second most frequent word used at Bruton. 'Talk to my parents and teachers' was quoted most at Bruton.

"Alice and I realised that we had a problem here. We wanted to devise a package of resources that would feed into our weekly tutor programme working with our senior school girls, developing some of these skills. We felt we had a window of opportunity around May, where we had five or six weeks where we could implement this project. While we were thinking about this, it coincided with quite a lot of media interest in The Chimp Paradox.[3] We used this research, alongside the reports we'd got from our surveys, and used this as the basis of the programme.

"We thought it was really important to work with the girls in a practical way and identify practical solutions to the problems they faced. Additionally, we wanted to underpin quite a lot of what we were doing with science, so we included that, and in the first session that we did with our girls we included some basic information regarding the brain. We focused on mostly Years 9 and 10, because we felt that wasn't a pinch point generally. The feedback we had was that was where their resilience and their ability to deal with failure became a problem.

"One of the things that we found is that procrastination is a real issue for them. We're also going to look at what are the strengths which aren't academic – a lot of our girls view academic success as the be all and the end all."

Lisa Moyle (Badminton) continued. "The great thing about this project is that it was a collaboration between Bruton and Badminton. At Badminton we wanted to explore the teacher perspective, to see how we presented ourselves to the girls and how we interacted with them.

"There was one thing which really struck a resonance with us, struck a chord, and it was this. We asked teachers who had the biggest influence

---

3. The Chimp Paradox is a mind management model designed by the psychiatrist Steve Peters and detailed in his book of the same name.

on girls and by far they felt that the peers, their parents or themselves were the biggest influencers. But when we asked the students whose opinion they valued the most when it came to their school work or what they did, it was crystal clear that it was what the teachers said which mattered to them. We thought this was quite a big discrepancy. As teachers, we had thought the importance of their peers, the importance of their friends, but for the girls it was much more important what the teachers felt.

"As professionals, therefore, we are much more influential than we give ourselves credit for. We need to think carefully how we feed back and how we interact with our students in order to get the best possible out of them. Our responses impact their resilience and what they do.

"We then asked each group to rank the following in terms of importance.

- Being clever.
- Being hardworking.
- My appearance.
- How popular I am.
- Being able to deal with setbacks.

"Whereas pupils ranked being hardworking, being clever and being able to deal with setbacks as being important, the teachers felt that girls would highlight being clever. Some of that is reflected in the type of school that we work in. Teachers felt that resilience was way down the list of importance for girls, but this wasn't the case. There was a clear mismatch between what the girls felt and what we as teachers thought they felt.

"With the next questions, in retrospect, we should probably have put the same question to the girls as to the teachers, but we asked it slightly differently. For the teachers, we asked 'Who puts the most pressure on the girls to achieve?'

- Themselves.
- Teachers.
- Parent(s)/family.
- Peers.

"Teachers said it was definitely the girls themselves that apply the pressure, followed by their parents. When we asked the pupils 'Overall, what do you think your teachers care most about?' ...

- You enjoying the subject.
- Preparing you for exams.
- Helping you learn exam techniques.
- Helping you learn more about the subject.
- Helping you become more confident as a person.

... it was 'preparing you for exams', then 'helping you learn more about the subject'. 'Helping you become more confident as a person' came bottom, which was quite impactful for us.

"In the next question, we asked pupils 'Which is the most important aspect of school?'

- The exam grades you achieve at the end.
- Friendships made at school.
- Extracurricular activities.
- Learning about a range of different subjects.
- Preparing for later life.

"This one shone through. Pupils said what was most important was preparation for later life, which was twice as important as exam grades. We're talking about girls from the age of 13 to 18. Ironically, none of them felt that extracurricular activities were the most important, and comparatively few felt friendships were the most important. Understanding that friendships and extracurricular are part of preparing for later life is something that we are going to have to teach our girls. They don't seem to value so much the relational side of school and we have a job of work as teachers to help them see and understand just how important that is for later life."

Lucy Griffith (Badminton) then talked about the survey that was delivered to teachers. "We asked: 'Do you feel perfectionism is a problem among your students?' The responses were in prose, it wasn't evaluated statistically. I read all the comments and tried to see if I could see any trends or patterns emerging from them, and synthesise the very thoughtful responses we got from colleagues about this issue of perfectionism. Crucially, pretty much everyone thought it was a problem – it was an issue in our girls' schools. What I then thought was very interesting is that the girls have kind of got this message about resilience, that it's OK to fail, and yet we still have this problem of perfectionism. One of the things that our colleagues are saying is that this is because we are saying one thing as schools but we are doing quite another.

"We say it's OK for you to fail, but departments are under such pressure to get exam results that as soon as they do fail we say, 'There's a clinic for you to go to.'

"We say it's important for wellbeing and success to have a work-life balance, yet we fill their lunch hours with clinics if they're not doing very well. We feel under pressure to market our school, to have lots of events which we want the girls to buy into. We don't monitor their time, so they're rushed off their feet. We're saying that we don't want them to be perfectionists. Have we got a culture which is in fact pushing them towards it and are we really celebrating other aspects apart from exam success? In our further discussion, we had wondered if ourselves as staff are guilty of a kind of perfectionism, and in the way that we appraise staff the complete focus on exam success means that we are buying into that perfectionist culture that we are saying doesn't work.

"There's a problem at the heart of our education system, which is basically that we have perhaps been pulled by our own anxieties as professionals in schools away from real educational values. We know that perfectionism isn't the answer. Does our system actually engender it? These are big strategic questions that senior leaders need to ask in our schools. As girls' schools, we should be taking a lead on this.

"How could this actually be moved forward? It seems to me we should look at how our students are spending their time and this could be researched for future leadership programmes. It would be interesting to track girls and see what we're doing to them with all these initiatives and things, and whether there is a work-life balance and whether we should have some responsibility for that. It would be interesting as well to see what happens to our students after school. If they achieve all their brilliant grades but don't flourish at university or flourish in the workplace, that means we're not doing our jobs right – not just to measure end-of-school success, but five years after.

"And if teachers are so important, it's important that our teachers are not stressed out, that they have the time and the capacity to spend quality time with the students that they mentor. We know our teachers are very influential, therefore we need to make sure that they can do that most valued job to the best of their ability."

From the reaction in the room, it was clear that the presentation had resonated strongly with the audience. Significantly, one of our corporate guests, Janet Thomas, a former president of Women in Banking and Finance, said: "I can think of a number of organisations I work with who would be interested in this research."

You can watch the Bruton/Badminton presentation in full at https://youtu.be/mAqo4Iw5T_w

The Canadian writer Toko-pa Turner has her own perspective on the problem of perfectionism:

"Perfectionism is one of the great pillars of patriarchy, used to stem the rise of the wild feminine … it is an impossible standard that, when we strive for it, guarantees our failure because it's ultimately unreachable. Perfection is a counterfeit form of beauty which, as you're strengthening your instincts, will ring with dissonance despite its seductive surface.

"True beauty always contains a delicious dash of chaos. It has a wild or unpredictable quality that takes you by surprise. Perfectionism tries to stamp out that quality in pursuit of an impeccability that strips a thing of its spontaneity. If we are seduced by it, it can choke all the life from our offering, turning it homogeneous and agreeable."

Case study #2: Readaxation

We faced another challenge to the design of the programme in Birmingham, where we had three participants. Tracy Goodyear and Hannah O'Rourke were from neighbouring state schools, King Edward VI Handsworth School for Girls and Handsworth Wood Girls' Academy, respectively. Rachael Speirs was from Saint Martin's School in Solihull, a small independent school a few miles away. They all taught English.

Having interviewed and profiled each of them, I decided it made sense to put them together as a trio for the purpose of the community project. It wasn't long before Hannah was in touch:

"Rachael and I met yesterday and following a lovely tour of Saint Martin's School, we decided that we are going to focus on the reading habits of 16+ students for our joint project.

"Between now and January, when Rachael will visit HWGA, we will research into the benefits of reading for 16+ students; exploring the reading habits of year 12 and 13 students within our own schools, paying particular attention to the idea of 'reading for pleasure' and the link between reading and the effect on one's mental health. As well as gathering articles, we intend to conduct questionnaires and surveys, with the use of social media to gain feedback from a wider audience. Furthermore, discussions with colleagues will also deepen our understanding on what students are reading, the variations in academic ability between avid readers and those who hardly read at all, and what motivates post-16 students to read. We will look to produce a paper detailing our findings.

"Finally, any strategies that we come across to improve reading habits or that emerge from our research we will trial and discuss outcomes."

By May 2018, the project had progressed sufficiently for the trio to present their work so far to the Sandhurst conference.

Rachael told the delegates: "We are all English teachers and we decided we wanted to do something to do with English. We then started to think about the stresses on teenagers and the emphasis on mental health and wellbeing. This is when we began our research and we began looking at articles by the Varkey Foundation, which had been researching why and where teenagers feel happy in the world. Britain unfortunately came quite low. We then looked at Young Minds research as well and began to look at the link between reading and wellbeing and positiveness and mental health.

"From that point we created a questionnaire, and asked about 170 of our sixth-form students to fill in information generally about their wellbeing: what made them happy, what made them sad, but then also linking to how much they read and whether that had any influence. From that point forwards we then collated those results, looked at that alongside our research, and began to think about what resources we could create that would begin what we then called a 'Readaxation' programme. Readaxation[4] is a term first used by Nicola Morgan, so we were in touch with her and she was quite happy for us to use that term."

In a later conversation, Rachael told me: "Our hope, unfortunately scuppered by Covid-19, was to involve the central library in Birmingham, hosting an event for teenage girls regarding reading and how it has huge benefits for positive mental health. The plan was also to produce a Readaxation programme that schools could use to examine the links between reading and mental health, signposting those in their care to materials that will relax and enhance their positive outlook, and therefore contribute to coping with the academic pressures and resilience needed during sixth form.

"Our findings were clear in that British teenagers clearly do struggle more with their mental health than many of their global counterparts, so this is something that continues to need addressing in schools and society. Another key finding and conclusion was that if you can engage teenagers in reading, it definitely does benefit them and contributes to positive mental health, more resilience and a general ability to cope better. However, that engagement is sometimes difficult to achieve, given the all-encompassing social media world that teenagers are surrounded by today. In addition, in my opinion, schools need to do much more as pupils begin their secondary education, or even in Years 5 and 6, to continue to inspire girls and especially boys with their reading, before they lose the enthusiasm that dominates in the early years."

I asked Rachael what she had learned, through working on the Readaxation project, from her colleagues in the state sector about the different opportunities and pressures they face.

"It's been really interesting, because we hadn't met before and what's been really fantastic about the collaboration is that, apart from the Readaxation project, we've also talked about a variety of other issues

---

4. Reading to relax – see www.nicolamorgan.com/the-reading-brain/what-is-readaxation

that face us in schools, and there are some different challenges based on socioeconomic background or other such differences. What we've actually found is that we've got a lot more in common. Obviously we're all girls' schools, so the things that girls find difficult to deal with in everyday life are pretty much the same across all three schools. That was something that we found quite pleasing, because there was a real point of common interest – we could help girls of whatever background and social identity they have. The stresses and strains of our teenage girls are pretty similar, living in Britain today."

6. Godolphin and Latymer conference, May 2019

In Bright Field's work with organisations ranging from large corporations to schools in both the state and independent sectors, we frequently encounter rules-based cultures that are highly anachronistic. One German bank had rules that had been established during the Second World War and never revisited. The Church of England may be the most egregious example of hanging on to rules that date back many hundreds of years and are not fit for purpose today.

The Covid-19 crisis has intensified the process of challenging old rules, in that new processes and workplace practices have been needed to curb the spread of the virus. But before the pandemic it was not unusual for us to encounter organisations where more than 50% of rules were out of date. Challenging these rules, creating a framework with more appropriate and usually fewer parameters, is key to unlocking the creativity innate in most organisations. At an individual client level, challenging one's own assumptions and those of the organisation is something we frequently do as coaches or mentors.

Buoyed by the success of the Sandhurst conference in 2018, we began planning a second event. We were keen to see how we might improve on the experience that the delegates had enjoyed. We weren't sure we could match the venue, but when we embarked on planning the event, things started to fall into place. We secured Godolphin and Latymer School in London as our venue, and the actor Juliet Stevenson agreed to be one of our keynote speakers. We also signed up Captain Mel Robinson, who later became the Navy's first female Commodore Maritime Reserves, and Kim Jarred, whose short film *My Baby* shares her experience of her child's early gender transition.

We had decided that the theme for the conference would be "challenging assumptions". Many of the mentees had told us that their own assumptions had been a constraint on their thinking when contemplating promotion. Conversations with their mentors had been crucial in helping to demolish those assumptions, as though a barrier had been knocked down and now they could reach the space beyond, allowing new possibilities to emerge.

The walls of Godolphin and Latymer's Victorian hall, where our conference took place, are unambiguously aspirational. A century of achievement is presented along their full length, through wooden boards inscribed with the names of students borne on scholarships to the distinguished colleges of Oxford and Cambridge, Harvard and Yale. The current generation of students may sit at the tables and wonder, "What would my name look like up there?"

Dr Frances Ramsey, head of Godolphin and Latymer, opened the conference. You may remember from the introduction that a conversation between Frances and me in 2016, when she was headmistress of Queen's College, London, had been instrumental in the creation of the mentoring programme. Harking back to our earlier discussion, she told the delegates: "While we look for vision in our colleagues, I did not anticipate that, three years on, we would be celebrating the achievements of the first cohort and embarking on a second group of future leaders."

Insights from Captain Mel Robinson

Mel was our first keynote speaker. At the time, she was deputy assistant chief of staff of the Maritime Reserves. In full uniform, looking every inch the military leader, she struck an imposing figure. Some overnight political news added a dramatic touch: Penny Mordaunt had been appointed the first female defence secretary and Mel thus found herself in the unique position of her new boss also being a subordinate. "That's just the most extraordinary thing – Penny is a sub-lieutenant [in the Royal Naval Reserve]," Mel told the delegates. "That will cause a bit of a problem, so we will have to have that conversation!"

She went on to tell the story of her naval career, and her struggle to retain a sense of self inside the organisation: "I have unashamedly modelled myself on other people – there were no female role models for me to model myself on in the Navy. I'm authentic by design. I chose my leadership style and designed it to fit into an institution.

"I'm a person in transition. I'm my biggest critic and my ability to consciously self-reflect is a skill I have taught and is the jewel in my crown.

"I can't tell you how challenging it was to retain an essence of self and an essence of myself when I first entered Britannia Naval College. You walk in as a civilian and remove your civilian clothes. You are given a number and a rank and you cease immediately to be the person that you were when you walked in through the gate. The institution was immediately looking to impose its own values and traditions, and to mould me into the leader that it thought it wanted me to be.

"The Navy knew they wanted to have a career structure for women, but that had no detail behind it. It didn't have anything designed into it that could help me or them actually track women through the system. I made it more complicated: I didn't just want to be designed into that pathway. I knew that I wanted children. I happened to marry a serviceman. So every step I took into the Navy, the more complicated it got.

"I've been bullied. I've been harassed. I've been challenged by my organisation. I've complained. I would encourage you to challenge your organisations when they're not doing for you what you should rightfully expect as women in these organisations. If I wasn't thriving in the organisation, I would leave."

Mel made history when she took command of HMS *Express* in 1998. "As I was driving my ship (you drive a ship) out of Troon and coming to the narrowest point in the channel, one of my ship's crew came and offered me a bacon butty. I was being witnessed and filmed by the national press so I turned the ship around, I reberthed and I rebriefed the ship's company on what we were going to do next. I explained that whatever *that* was, it was not going to be the way that I would command the ship. It wasn't a normal command: people were watching my every move, waiting for me to have an accident, to have issues to demonstrate that women at sea was not a good thing."

In the run-up to the Godolphin and Latymer conference, Hilary, with 30 years of school productions and wardrobe design behind her, had asked Mel whether she would be more comfortable presenting as Captain or civilian. They had come up with the idea of a costume change to take place during Mel's speech.

Mel continued: "In order to give you a real sense as to who I am, and to give you a real sense of the person behind this transformation, I have to give you a little bit more of myself. And that means that I start to lose the real sense of Captain Mel Robinson, because as much as the uniform's important to me, it's not the be all and end all." She removed her captain's jacket and placed it neatly on the nearby chair.

"I'm going to talk a bit about changing my leadership style now – it was as much about standing out as a leader as it was fitting in." Mel removed her tie, which joined the jacket on the chair as she undid the top button of her shirt.

"Sometimes it's useful to start reshaping myself." She untucked the shirt from her trousers, to supportive chuckles from the room. "I'm already feeling more comfortable – it's bizarre, isn't it?"

Next, Mel took off her shoes and put on a pair of heels. "I'm feeling more comfortable because I don't like flat shoes – I love a heel!"

Warming to her theme, she said, "I've been in envy of you all morning." More laughter from the smartly dressed colleagues. "Isn't it funny, as I'm already feeling more comfortable because I'm losing the constraints of the uniform. I'm able to have an honest conversation with you.

"I said it was very important to maintain an essence of yourself, and that's quite difficult to achieve in an environment where values are being inflicted on you. When I fell pregnant with my son, there were so few women in the service that we did not and we had not contracted a maternity uniform. So when I was pregnant, to the extent that my baby couldn't be engulfed in that uniform, they took it off me and I went in civilian clothes. When I left the service to have my son, I had a real issue with that. What I came to realise was that I had credited the essence of myself to my uniform and I'd forgotten that I wasn't made in the Navy – contrary to the current recruiting ads. I'd *joined* the Navy.

"It took me a long time to come to terms with the fact that I had been reckless enough to give my values away to a uniform. I had to go through some personal counselling to get myself back to a space where I got my self-esteem back. I lost a bit of myself in that process. I talk about forgiving the service for some of the terrible things it's done to me – that was one of the worst." She pointed at her discarded uniform on the chair. "I'm really glad I put that uniform over there now.

"I didn't make that mistake when I went back into service and I've kept that part of me disconnected. What I want to say to anybody is that there are two parts of me: there's Captain Mel Robinson and there's Mel Robinson the person. Most of the time I can integrate the two and bring them together in one place, but sometimes you'll feel me quite disconnected and you'll hear it in my language. But the Navy did that to me and I will work quite hard to make sure they don't do that to anybody else.

"I want to talk to you about Phoenix. The conversation I had with Ian when we were planning today was about Phoenix Rising. It's about understanding whether I want to fit in or whether I want to stand out." To make the point, Mel put on a bright pink cardigan. "I came to learn in my journey that it was as much about fitting in as standing out. In the military, when I'm not in my uniform, I'm known to have very pretty bags and I wear very bright colours. There is part of me that's wanting to bring my femininity to that military organisation.

"Phoenix – this moment of coming to this point of renewal – taught me that my employer hasn't always been kind, hasn't always treated me well. It hasn't managed my talents. I've managed my talent myself. I've owned my journey. It hasn't recognised my achievements. It may promote me to Commodore Maritime Reserves,[5] it may not, and I had to ask myself: is this femininity valuable to the Navy? I think it is. But are the traits and beliefs I've described to you? Do I have to stay in the military to have an impact now? Or is it time for me to step away from that institution and think about what I do next? I'm 50 years old, so I have another 10 to 15 years' work in me. I'm not quite sure whether I want to spend it in the Navy."

5. Mel was promoted to Commodore in February 2020.

In just a few moments, Mel had transformed, in full view of the audience, from a military leader into a woman who happened to work as a leader in a military organisation.

Conference delegate and mentee Catherine Hitchen was eager to know whether, if she had her time again, Mel would go into the Navy. "Yes, I would," Mel replied. "I realised that the Admiralty was very committed to working with women, it just didn't have enough women in senior positions to know how they were going to make it work. So I have absolutely no regrets, because every step I took changed something and made it a little bit easier for the women that were following behind. I think I've been given an opportunity to blend legacies into the Navy with my work and my passions, which means that I can live and experience a very different journey."

Jane Lunnon, who was then head of Wimbledon High School in London, picked up the theme of authenticity in her question to Mel: "How do you stay true to yourself, especially when there's no one else in the organisation being that person? How do you reflect the needs of the role without becoming a caricature of yourself?"

Mel responded: "You come back to your core values, as opposed to the organisation's values, because at some stage there may be a conflict. I've never had an issue with the Navy's values, I just happen to think that what I added on top of them made me even more special. I think my journey makes me unique; the essence of me and the values and how I learned to apply them in the organisation make me exclusive. So I'm now exclusive in an inclusive organisation – a relatively inclusive organisation.

"The key point around authenticity was accepting that not everyone likes me. Once you accept that some people don't like aspects of you, you're even more comfortable to own that. There's no falseness about it.

"Stanley McChrystal, the US Army General, said leadership is a process of influencing a group toward some defined outcome, but he redefines it and challenges myths around leadership: 'Leadership is a complex system of relationships between leaders and followers, in a particular context, that provides meaning to its members.' I'm seeking to take my leadership in the military and recontextualise it into something else. What was most telling about that was that he also talked about leaders being symbolic.

I'm very visible in the organisation: there are only two women captains in Reserve and 12 across the Navy, so when a female captain does walk into the room, *she does walk into the room*. What I'm told by the junior ladies in the organisation is that symbol is very powerful for them. In terms of being a role model, it's really important that you own your responsibility for that on a daily basis."

On the screen behind Mel, the image switched from a uniformed McChrystal to a distinctly un-uniformed Dolly Parton. The quote read, "If your actions create a legacy that inspires others to dream more, learn more, do more and become more, then you are an excellent leader."

Mel concluded: "I accept I'm a role model. I accept that I'm introducing the Navy mentoring programme, which will be my legacy for leaders that will follow me in many years to come. You've heard me talk about my passions. Where I have been most effective in my career is where I've been very synergised with my passions and doing what I love. I would encourage you to find out what your passions are and go with them.

"I want you to hold the parts of you that are closest to you – your values. Protect them and nurture them. Don't ever give them away, because that sense of me dedicating myself to an organisation instead of me took a long time to get over.

"Every time I step into the room I have to be on top of my game. Your brand is what other people say about you when you're not in the room. Brand that is aligned with your behaviours helps you to behave in predictable ways. People will describe me as driven and purposeful, but I would always want people to see Captain Mel Robinson walk out of the room and have a sense that she cared for them as individuals within the organisation."

You can watch Mel's speech in full at https://youtu.be/xfncayu2mkE

Insights from Juliet Stevenson

I have known Juliet since 1995, when we met through the London International Festival of Theatre, in which we were both involved. I was due to interview her at the Godolphin and Latymer conference and, several weeks beforehand, I sent her an outline script highlighting three roles from her career that I thought would be interesting to explore in the context of women's lives and leadership.

The first of these roles was Paulina in Ariel Dorfman's *Death and the Maiden*, which Juliet performed at the Royal Court in the early 1990s. The play, set in an unnamed country that resembles Pinochet's Chile, tells the story of a former political prisoner who was tortured and raped by her captors, led by a man whose face she never saw. Years after the country's dictatorship has fallen, Paulina encounters a stranger and recognises his voice as that of her rapist. Juliet won an Olivier Award for her performance.

On stage at the conference, I asked Juliet about this performance. She said: "I felt for the first time ever in my working life that it was not possible to imagine what it was like to be systematically raped and tortured every day – it was not an imaginable thing. I felt like a fraud – as an actor your job is to imagine everything, but that was just beyond imagination.

"I also felt a very strong sense of responsibility, because I knew that out there, all over the world, there are people that have endured this. You have such a responsibility to tell their story truthfully; it's much bigger than any of us, than any play we might be doing. I was very daunted and I went to find Helen Bamber. She was an astonishing woman who, as a young nurse with the Red Cross, first saw the survivors of those Nazi concentration camps ... Subsequently, she joined Amnesty and then started the Medical Foundation for the Care of Victims of Torture, now called Freedom From Torture. She introduced me to this extraordinary community of Chilean refugees in London. They were phenomenal women, but still struggling with the repercussions of that experience. They explained that when you are being tortured, if you survive – which, of course, many didn't – it's because you've found a way of separating yourself from your body. So you literally cut yourself off from this thing which is in such pain and is being so abused, and you literally leave it. One of the jobs of those trying to heal people is to marry the person back into their body again, but that is an extremely complicated process. For many women it's not fully achieved."

Also in the early 1990s, Juliet played Nina in Anthony Minghella's film *Truly, Madly, Deeply*. Nina is grieving the loss of her partner, Jamie, played by Alan Rickman, who returns as a ghost.

After conference delegates viewed a short clip from the film, Juliet explained: "The reason Anthony wanted to write this piece is that everybody's life contains loss. Its representation in film and on stage has often been glamourised: you see the one exquisite tear rolling down the heroine's face, but she still looks great. I felt that when you're experiencing loss, you don't feel good. You feel revolting. You feel anger. You feel hurt, depressed, hopeless, ugly, overweight. You don't feel good about any part of yourself and I think it's important to tell those stories."

The third role I wanted to discuss was Rosalind Franklin in the 1987 film *Life Story*. Franklin was a brilliant scientist whose work was critical to the discovery of the structure of DNA in the early 1950s. Before becoming a research associate at King's College London in 1951, Franklin had worked in Paris, where women enjoyed a more equal working relationship with men than was the case in London. At King's, women were not allowed in the common room, which was a bastion of male exclusivity.

Of Franklin, Juliet observed: "She found post-war London very oppressive, very chauvinistic, and very patronising towards women in her profession, and so she was very unhappy.

"There are so many gender issues bound into her story ... Working in an entirely male institution, with 'male' methodology, she seemed to have repressed the instinctive capacity for scientists to make leaps. They proceed very minutely with their research data, but then apparently in scientific discovery there are these moments of imagination and instinct – that's very often where a huge discovery is made. She seemed to have suppressed that."

It was only when Juliet and I spoke a week before the conference that she highlighted the connection between these three roles. "Each of them has to contend with being isolated as a woman," she said. "Paulina was a victim of torture and rape, Nina was isolated with grief, and Rosalind had been marginalised by her male colleagues."

The more I thought about it, the more the theme of isolation applies to many of the leaders we coach. Senior staff members in schools and other organisations are frequently left without colleagues to refer to or confer with, especially on delicate matters. They often face tough decisions and would benefit from a second opinion or a trusted colleague to bounce ideas around with.

Juliet said: "The three characters unite in your mind. In *Death and the Maiden* there is a sense of utter isolation. Women can't talk about rape very often, which is why all the statistics are misguided and never reflect the reality in terms of numbers. But women's relationship to their real sexuality, even before and outside rape, is something which many women carry isolatedly. We think we talk to our women friends, and maybe we do, but we don't often tell the full story. In a situation where a woman has been raped and tortured and never been able to speak of it, even to her loving husband, is a story of isolation. In *Truly, Madly, Deeply*, grief has the same impact. They are three different women, but not having the language to speak of their experience, not having a culture which recognises their experience, not having the systems that reflect their experience are all things which they have in common."

You can watch Juliet's interview at https://youtu.be/Hao0krQt1Pk

Insights from Kim Jarred

Of all the issues facing school leaders, aside from Covid-19, the questions arising from gender are probably the most challenging. Keeping with our theme of "challenging assumptions", Hilary and I had asked Kim Jarred, whom we had known for a long time, to speak about her journey. After learning that her child wished to transition, Kim made a short film about the experience. We took the view that her story would be a powerful and important one to share with our audience.

Here's an extract from her speech at the conference.

"I live in Woking in Surrey with my husband and two children. *My Baby* is my first film. I didn't make a conscious decision to make a film, I really had no idea that I was going to. I had often thought I'd quite fancy making one, a bit like when people say they have a book inside them, but I never really knew what to make a film about, never knew what my story would be. And then one day, I found that I had a story to tell.

"It's coming up for three years since our eldest child, our 10-year-old daughter, told us she wished to live as boy. I'd be lying if I said it was a complete surprise, because there'd been many clues which I'd tried to brush away, but it was still an enormous thing to get our heads around when the words were finally said: 'Mummy, I feel like a boy inside.'

For years and years I'd been the mother of a girl, and with that had assumed all kinds of futures for my daughter and dreamed the dreams that mothers often dream: girly shopping trips, sharing secrets about first boyfriends, watching them get married and knitting for their babies. To be fair, with this 'extreme tomboy' we lived with, it didn't look like things were heading that way at all, but a mum can still dream. Perhaps it was just a 'tomboy phase'? Looking back, I felt quite stupid that I hadn't seen what was right before my eyes.

"My daughter transitioned to living as a boy rapidly, at her request. After all, she had been waiting a long time to do it – three to four years, in her words. Three to four years in which it seemed we had all been unknowingly living a lie. Almost immediately, we bought new 'boy' clothes and the already short hair became very short hair. Within four months she was a full-time boy, with new pronouns and a new name.

"It was quite astonishing how quickly it all happened once the floodgates had been opened. I've read plenty of discussions and disagreements about parents being overly permissive in these circumstances, or even rushing their children through the process at unacceptable speed. Lots of people seem to have lots of opinions – mostly people who have never been through it, I might add. But I can tell you, when your child tells you something so monumental and with such clarity, you listen and you listen hard.

"To suggest that parents could push a child down this trickiest of paths is unthinkable. The things my child told me that had been going around in their head demonstrated a depth of self-awareness which was frankly breathtaking. We had no reason to doubt what he was feeling and so let him lead the way at his own pace. He forged his own path with great courage and has never once looked back or faltered, despite the many challenging situations he had to face.

"So, we now had two sons and no daughter. To say it was overwhelming would be an understatement. We were feeling completely out of our depth. While relieved at finally being who he wanted to be, our son sobbed often at night, wishing he had a different body, threatening to cut parts off and desperate to grow a beard. We played amateur therapists as best we could. Apart from wholeheartedly supporting him, we didn't really know what to do next. Actual professional help for transgender children is very hard to access – the current waiting time for being seen at the Gender Identity Development Service at the Tavistock is 20 months. At the time we were referred, it was a 10-month wait, which was still a very, very long time when you have a child in need.

"We owe a huge debt of thanks to the charity Mermaids, who were our greatest support during this time. We were able to go on a residential weekend where we met other families with transgender children, and finally we didn't feel so alone. My son was thrilled to meet other transgender children of all ages and was able to be himself, free, uninhibited and without worrying whether he 'passed' as a boy or not.

"While I was 100% supportive of all my son was going through, inside I was struggling hugely with the enormity of the change that had happened. My feelings were very complex and mixed up about the past and the future. About eight months after he had made his announcement about his true feelings, I got up very early one morning. I literally had no idea I was going to do this, but I started to write a poem. I have never written poetry in my life before, so I clearly had the need to offload some thoughts. The words poured out of me and they wouldn't stop until I'd written the story from beginning to end.

"A week later, I read it out to a group of friends and, as I did so, I realised I was seeing moving pictures alongside it. Before I'd even voiced that, a very wise friend said something along the lines of: 'That would make a really beautiful film.' And thus, a ball started to roll.

"Within a few months, a friend had put me in touch with my producer, Andy Linfield, and with his guidance I had written a script of sorts. He put together a small team to work with, we cast the parts, and I threw out a plea to family and friends to help me fund the crazy idea of making a film. Seven months after I wrote the poem, on a tiny budget, we shot the film locally in a weekend. It was possibly the most terrifying and stressful two days of my whole life. Flying by the seat of my pants would be a good way of explaining it!

"I assumed, naively, that once the careful plans were in place it would all go smoothly, but so many things did not go to plan. I had literally no idea how to direct a film and was performing the jobs of about

10 people, but I did have a clear vision in my head and somehow we managed to do it. I'm eternally grateful for the gift of Ana Nunes, my cinematographer, who captured the essence of what I wanted so beautifully, and worked so hard with the editing to get the final cut the way I wanted it. Additionally, I was blessed with a beautiful cast who, without fuss, took my haphazard instructions and pulled off great performances in front of the camera. We did it and I'm so proud of what we've achieved.

"Over the last couple of years, one of the things my son and I have done is connect with other people in the transgender community. We went to our first Pride in London a year after he transitioned. We took part in the parade, marching with other families and their children. It was frankly a complete gamechanger in the way my son perceived himself. Before Pride he felt an outsider; he didn't really fit anywhere and he felt different. At Pride, we found there was not only acceptance out there in the world and a huge amount of support, but even better – and I believe this to be the most important factor – there was actual celebration of difference.

"My 11-year old son paraded, sang, even danced through the crowded streets, his confidence buoyed by being with his tribe. He waved his big trans flag, he high-fived people, and he embraced people in the crowds. It was very emotional, as a parent, to watch. Here I could see, plainly, in action, the reason Pride celebrations exist. Pride empowered him, made him feel everything ultimately could be OK in his world. His future looked brighter as he felt connected to his community. In a world which is not always kind and tolerant, being able to celebrate who you are can make a whole lot of difference to your self-esteem and identity.

"I hope that what I have created brings a deeper and more compassionate understanding of the subject of transgender children and their families. I challenge people while watching the film to think about their current assumptions about the trans community, trans children and gender in general, and where these assumptions may have come from. Do those around you in your work have the same or different assumptions? And are there things you might want to think about differently moving forward?"

You can watch Kim's film and her conference speech here: https://youtu.be/mWgP6bTcZvk

7. Racism and gender bias

It's Friday 5 April 1968. I'm in the school hall at Bellevue Junior High School, just outside Seattle in the State of Washington, US. My family moved here in 1966 when my father got a job with Boeing. I'm now in the eighth grade and my English accent has given way to something that I'm told sounds vaguely Canadian.

It is the day after Dr Martin Luther King Jr has been assassinated. We schoolchildren are expecting that our assembly this morning will contain some reference to the killing. Mostly, though, we are looking forward to the forthcoming holiday.

Our principal, Mr Phelps, strides to the podium. Donald Phelps[6] has been in charge for less than a year, but in that time he has established a positive following among the students and teachers for his welcoming demeanour and the clarity of his leadership. What singles him out is that he is the only Black person in the school. His grandfather was one of the first Black residents in Seattle, arriving in 1888 from Mississippi.

Looking around the hall, Mr Phelps is silent for a moment. He then begins to speak, wishing us well for the holiday. As his address draws to a close, his voice grows stronger, not needing the microphone that has been provided. "When you go home today," he says, "I want you to ask your parents one question." He pauses. "Am I a second-class citizen merely because I'm a Black man?"

I glance around. You could hear a pin drop. One or two staff members are weeping openly; others are drying their eyes. The rest of the day

---

6 You can read more about Donald Phelps here: www.blackpast.org/african-american-history/phelps-donald-g-1929-2003

passes in a blur and I recount the assembly to my parents when I get home. My father says I am fortunate to have such a man as my principal.

Many years later, when I am working for Barclays, I organise an off-site day for some colleagues. Our facilitator takes us through a questionnaire designed to highlight some of our personality differences. One of the questions asks whether an interracial relationship would be more challenging for the couple than a relationship between two people of the same ethnic background. There are eight of us in the room, seven of whom reply that we see no difference. My own reaction when reading the question was that to have answered otherwise might have been perceived as racist.

The only dissenter is a White colleague whose husband is African Asian. "I know where you may be coming from," she says, "but it is a very challenging relationship." As she tells her story, I can see that the reactions of colleagues echo those of my classmates in 1968. They are witnessing first-hand, and almost certainly for the first time, powerful and authentic testimony that goes to the heart of the everyday experience of prejudice. From the conversations that take place immediately afterwards, it is clear that their perceptions of racism have been transformed by this experience.

In this chapter, we will address two aspects of prejudice. First, we will hear from the former headteacher Floyd Steadman about his experiences of racial bias in education and in his earlier sporting career. Later, we will hear from Gwen Byrom and Lucy Giles on the issue of gender bias in education and how to improve leadership development practices.

When writing the book *Heads Up: the challenges facing England's leading head teachers* (2013), Dominic Carman interviewed Diana Ellis of the recruitment firm Odgers Berndtson. He asked Ellis, cited as the "leading headhunter for independent school heads", whether there would be more headteachers from ethnic minorities in 20 years' time. She replied: "I wouldn't think we would rush to do that, because what people are buying is British education, and therefore they want to see a British leader."

Alarmingly, this view is still manifest today. In 2020, one of our participants in the mentoring programme was considering applying for a headship. A recruitment firm (not Odgers Berndtson) had been mandated to help with the selection. The school in question has a multi-ethnic board of governors and includes in its values "Respect others regardless of age, background or race". Despite this, our colleague, who is of mixed heritage, was told by the recruiter that she "wouldn't pass the Governor's Speech Day Test". Not being familiar with this phrase, she sought clarification, only to be told that the combination of her experience, current school and education would render her inappropriate for the role.

Another Bright Field client, Nick Dennis, is looking to remedy the recruitment process and his work is informing the efforts of the Girls' Schools Association and the Independent Schools Council to attract more diverse candidates for teaching and board positions. Nick is focusing on streamlining the recruitment process to increase applications, while reducing potential for bias. He also suggests that institutions use a multitude of media channels to advertise posts, with targeted channels for a variety of demographics, and explore the use of an employee referral scheme as an additional recruitment strategy.

Insights from Floyd Steadman

Floyd Steadman has had a long and distinguished career in education. He has been headteacher of several independent schools and is now a part-time consultant working on headteacher appointments at Anthony Millard Consulting. Floyd also played senior rugby for Saracens FC for 10 years and is one of only 14 players inducted into the Saracens Hall of Fame.

I interviewed him in March 2021 about his extraordinary career and his experiences of racial prejudice.

When you were making your way in your teaching career, what did you find most challenging and how did you overcome that barrier?

"The biggest was the whole thing about unconscious bias and people making assumptions about me just on the colour of my skin. Because it's unconscious, they don't realise they're making those assumptions; their behaviours are based on assumptions and they don't really know that much about me. I felt people expected the work I produced as a teacher to be of a lower standard – they had lower expectations of me.

"I had some lucky breaks [in my life]. When I was in a children's home, the people who looked after the home were Betty and Fred – they were doing their best to protect me and I couldn't see it at the time. They were deliberately keeping me away from other, more challenging boys and now I understand why. I was 10, 11, 12.

"In my last year at school I was too old to stay in the children's home. My PE teacher, Brian Jones, who clearly knew my story (although I didn't think he did) – he kept saying to me, 'I've got a big house, you can rent a room in my house.' I was desperate, I had nowhere else to go, and eventually I said, 'Can I take you up on that?' In this day and age that would be unheard of, but the fact was I was doing it legitimately. I was basically renting a room in his house, and that was the year I got through my A-levels.

"At the same time as I was beginning to progress in rugby, there was a young PE teacher at my school, Gwen James, whose husband, Gareth, played for the great London Welsh team in the 1970s. He was kept out of the Welsh team and the British Lions team by one of his best mates, JPR Williams. Because of my rugby prowess at school, she introduced me to her husband and he introduced me to these London Welsh gods. I was there on the training pitch with people like JPR Williams, John Dawes, Gerald Davies, Mervyn Davies. Because I was just a teenage schoolboy, I didn't really understand that they were famous; now I can look back and say what a lucky young man I was to do that. At Christmas and other times, Gareth and Gwen would say, 'Come on over to spend some time with us, Floyd,' and it was people like that who really supported me though the most challenging and difficult of times."

Did you experience a difference between the way you were treated in sport and the way you were treated in education?

"In sport, there was disbelief that this Black young man, or boy, was playing scrum half number 9. Back in the mid to late 70s, early 80s, if you were a Black rugby player progressing through the ranks and becoming quite successful, you were either one of the outside backs, like Chris Oti, or you were one of the big forwards, like Victor Ubogu. A small, Black scrum half was unheard of. Someone asked me the other day, 'Has there been another top-class Black scrum half in England?' We struggled to think of another. There were people questioning whether I had the intellect to lead my team, to control the play, to liaise with the referee, to control the tempo of the game. The question was, 'Can this Black player do this? Can this Black man do this?' They were some of the challenges in rugby.

"Another challenge was the myth that Black players can run but they don't like physicality – the abuse that was dished out to me. The physical part of the game was the part that I loved. I just kept bouncing back.

"I can think of a number of games with teams like Pontypridd and Pontypool, Neath, Swansea and Llanelli – those teams would just kick me around the park. I would never, ever complain. I would just bounce back and get up smiling and say, 'Is that the best you've got?' That would really wind them up. We were all just dancing around, because what they were trying to do was to put me off my game, as the scrum half, as the playmaker, and I would retaliate in a very subtle way by trying to put them off *their* game. They were the challenges from the rugby field.

"In terms of education, the assumptions people were making were that I was not going to be as effective a teacher as potentially many others. The other challenge was the glass ceiling that you're trying to smash on the ladder to success – the stepping stone. If you were from a minority it was definitely harder."

Was there a point at which you felt you had progressed significantly in terms of your own persona?

"The answer to that is yes and no. Once you've become captain of Saracens and played for them for 10 seasons, and gone on to teach at the great St Paul's School, and yet there's still a little bit of impostor syndrome... All the way through to my first headship, there was that niggling doubt saying, 'Should I be doing this? Am I capable of doing this?' Of course I had the skill set, but there was that niggling doubt, and it wasn't until my second headship that I managed to put that away and say, 'I am good enough. I do have the skill set. I will do a good job.'"

Once you got to that point, what did you notice about what you were able to do that you couldn't previously?

"In my role as a senior manager, I managed to – and this is important – articulate with more clarity but also quite succinctly. I'm not one for waffle. You do have to have clarity and have direction, and I learned how to do that with confidence."

You spoke earlier about your experience of the glass ceiling. Have you ever framed that for a woman that you've been mentoring?

"No, I haven't, because it's only recently that I've been mentoring female heads. There is one in particular: she's an Oxford graduate, she's worked in the UK and overseas, she's a brilliant senior manager, and it's only recently that she's got her first headship. I've been working with her behind the scenes. It's about building her resilience and confidence, reassuring her that she does have the skill set, and making sure that at the right time she can impress the appropriate people. It's getting people to look beyond what they see – a Black woman, a Black man – and assess us for our skill set."

In terms of schools, what do you see as the most significant challenges in diversity and inclusion?

"One of the big challenges is the lack of diversity at the top. You and I know that there's a lot of pressure on boards now to be more diverse, and the boards understand that – they don't want to be accused of tokenism. If we're quite blunt, there isn't a big selection in the pool below – in effect, there probably has to be some tokenism done for the right reason. You're not picking someone to tick a box, you're picking someone that has the skill set. And if you take some flak, well, accept it, because you've done it with integrity and for the right reasons.

"In my firm there is a very broad acceptance and I've been very impressed. The chairman last summer invited me to talk to all the company by Zoom; he wanted me to be quite blunt and brutal, and give a flavour in the presentation of some of the challenges that I face. I've spoken about how I overcome them, and the feedback from board members was actually very moving.

"I see my job as kickstarting the conversation and making people aware of the challenge that minorities face, but I do it in a positive way. I know that a lot of the people that we need onside, if I'm negative or aggressive, we're going to lose them. My story is challenging and difficult, but actually there's a positive outcome. And I do it in a very non-threatening way. And that, I believe, is helping to kickstart the conversations that must be had. So the board have taken it on really well and my role then is, whenever possible, I'm representing my company by going out and speaking to others. When I speak to others about unconscious bias and the challenges I've faced, I'm representing Anthony Millard Consulting, and I've got their full backing and blessing to do that.

"I'm trying to open people's eyes to the fact that we all have unconscious biases, and they are going to impact on our lives and the lives of people around us. If we can just begin to understand some of our unconscious biases, maybe we can have a more positive impact on the people we meet."

What are you doing as a recruiter to address this?

"I see my role as two things. I'm helping with the recruitment of headteachers, and I think I can go in with a slightly different approach and make sure people aren't being rejected for the wrong reasons. I can challenge and say, 'This applicant we've got with an unusual name – what are the skill sets? Are we missing anything just because of the name?' But I think my most important role is the message when I go and lead presentations. I'm helping to kickstart the conversation, and with my background I think I have the authority to do that."

You're currently writing your autobiography. What are you hoping your book will deliver?

"I'm writing for two main reasons. Firstly, my late wife always said to me, 'You've got such an interesting story, you should write a book.' I'm doing it in honour of her. Secondly, I'm doing it because I think I can make a difference to youngsters who are coming up. Maybe they've got struggles and they don't know what to do and where to turn, and they use the fact that they're a person of colour – that's why it's all going against them and nothing's working. Well, actually, listen to my story, look where I started. I've been relatively successful – you can overcome the challenges. So I hope it will inspire some people."

Were there any role models, male or female, who inspired you?

"When I was younger I read stories about Harriet Tubman, and I also read about Mary Seacole – it's only recently that people know about her. She possibly did as much as Florence Nightingale, but she was unheard of for all this time. We all know about Rosa Parks and other historical Black women who did very courageous and brave things. The recent

Black woman who inspired me is Michelle Obama – the first African American to be First Lady. She must have had a lot of flak, but I thought that she carried herself so well, just like her husband carried himself so well. I understand that one of the many reasons why she behaved that way is you feel that you're a role model, a torchbearer, and if you get it wrong it's going to be harder for people who come up after you.

"Nelson Mandela, Muhammad Ali, Pelé and Dr Martin Luther King – when I was a Black teenager I needed those positive role models. On TV I remember Sidney Poitier – I can't think of any others.

"Within education at that time, I didn't have any Black male or female role models who were in senior management that I could look up to and say, 'I can do that.' I hope that by becoming a head, particularly in the independent sector, I inspired people: 'If he can do that, I can do that.'

"Headhunters and recruiters have a widespread role in supporting governing bodies to make senior appointments, particularly in the independent sector. But it is open to question whether they widen the pool of talent from which to choose, or whether they, consciously or otherwise, reinforce the status quo."

Insights from Gwen Byrom

Gwen Byrom, director of education strategy at NLCS International, was the GSA's 2018 president. She and I have talked at length about the issue of gender bias in education.

"When two-thirds of teachers are women and less than half of school leaders are women, we're getting something wrong," Gwen says. "There's a huge talent pool that is being missed. I don't think it's because women don't want the roles. I don't think it's because women aren't capable and I don't think it's much to do with a lack of confidence. I think it is to do, to a degree, with role-modelling, which is where coaching comes in. You need to see other successful women taking on these roles." This echoes Mel Robinson's comments in her conference speech (chapter 6).

"I think, for me, the place where all of this falls down is that we're not necessarily hitting the right people all the time. So we're hitting the middle and senior leaders heading up into headship at a senior role, and that's great.

"One of the things we need to do is to get, at a much earlier stage, career teachers as well. I had to work really hard with a member of my teaching staff at Loughborough [High School, where Gwen was head for seven years] who was a phenomenally good teacher. When a head of department role came up in the school that I felt she ought to go for, we had to work quite hard to convince her that she could do it. There is scope there for widening out for not just senior leaders."

For Gwen, a related theme is the quality of governance and selection panels. "Speaking as a woman who has applied for roles and leadership roles on numerous occasions, I think we fall down when it's about governance and panels, and when panels think they know what they're looking for," she says.

"It's great to get the women that we're getting looking at leadership and what their strengths and weaknesses are, and how we can coach them into where this is right for them and they feel they have the tools to make the next step. My big worry, and I've seen it a lot of times, is that people get the door closed in their face and all that confidence and belief starts to bleed away. They say, 'Maybe I'm not as good as I think I am. Maybe it isn't for me after all.' My big irritation is that some of it is to do with perceptions of what a leader is by those panels.

"There is a big degree of complacency in some governing bodies that they know what they're doing and nobody can tell them what to do. The number of panels I've sat in front of that have been all White, male, mid-50s. I've spoken to other headship candidates. I spoke to one the other day: she didn't get the job because they wanted somebody more 'charismatic'. What the hell is charisma? Or gravitas? Gravitas is a word which really annoys me. We're trying to break open this idea of what leadership looks like and that it doesn't have to be that archetypal description of: what does a head look like? There are so many people who are and could be phenomenal leaders, but they would do it in a slightly different way. They look different, they dress themselves differently and they would approach it differently. It doesn't mean it's wrong, but there is a fear among a number of governing bodies, particularly about breaking the mould and going to someone a bit different, just because they're naturally conservative by nature.

"Coaching can be such a valuable thing, but your needs develop over time. When you have secured a senior post, it's more important that you have that coach. What you need from them is different; you're looking at different things at that stage, at different people. We need to see this as an ongoing process, so that career coaching is embedded in all they do. Colleagues need to be much more confident to ask for it, so that once they're in a headship role, if they've had that coaching, they're quite comfortable to say, 'I've had this, I want this to continue.'

"In teaching, our career development structure is really shocking ... If you look at how the Army deals with taking people through a leadership structure and preparing people for leadership, it's not rocket science or earth-shattering. But we assume, because somebody's good in the classroom, that they'll be a good head of department, a good middle leader and then a senior leader. Often they're not, and we end up with people who are very unhappy because they were the best in the classroom.

"Lucy Giles and I did an interview for BBC Radio Berkshire recently. We were chatting about the Army's approach to development and how, when you start to progress up through the promotion ranks, you go on cadre courses to pursue skills of leadership. It's not mentoring, it's more functional than that, but the message Lucy gives is, 'You're going to be in command, you're going to be in command of this number of people, and these are the skills you will need in order to do that.' They [the Army] talent-spot and they move people up in a much more organised way than teaching, which relies on the tap on the shoulder."

Insights from Lucy Giles

Lucy Giles takes up the story. Recently promoted to Colonel, she is now president of the Army Officer Selection Board, focused on bringing young people with promise and potential through a series of development pathways.

"We talk a good game in terms of maximising talent, but nobody is explicitly telling us to do this," she says. "Now I spend a lot of my time identifying people who are great in a number of areas, although I wouldn't have done that a few years ago, because the culture didn't allow for that kind of flexible approach."

What triggered the change in culture?

"The thing that triggered a change in culture, for me, was when our senior generals launched the Army Leadership Code in 2015. That framework is about behaviours: who we are, what we do and how we do it. It was a massive precedent for the Army to do that. When it was published, it became a catalyst for change. It was post the findings from the Blake report into Deepcut [barracks], where we had lost five young soldiers to suicide in the 1990s, and which exposed a broader culture of bullying in our training establishments and regiments. While there will be some individuals that get things wrong in today's Army, the behaviour expected is unequivocal; the values need to be our moral compass. From 2011 onwards – when I moved on promotion to the Defence Academy of the UK, studying leadership – behaviour and military ethics was part of my role."

From what level or rank would you start to notice people?

"You can notice or identify talented people at every rank in the Army. If you have experienced that talent management yourself, you are in turn more comfortable about applying that in your own personal contacts. For example, the then Chief of General Staff, General Sir Nick Carter, selected me to go on a Remarkable Women programme in 2016. It was fantastic to be thought that I was worth that kind of investment! Inevitably it makes you want to do that for other people, and I spend a lot of my time doing that now.

"All of the female officer cadets that I had the privilege of training at Sandhurst were invited at the end of the course for a cup of tea or glass of something at my home. I would gather some of the other female instructors and we would have a chat to reinforce the importance of networks, how to have difficult conversations when you are in a minority group, and encourage them to think about their future as leaders. We now have a Sandhurst Sisterhood of over 3,500 members, all with the shared love of service and an understanding of what it's like to be a minority in the Army. It's a tight group and it's brilliant, with subjects ranging from 'How do I solve this problem?' to 'Anyone available for dog-sitting?'"

In the mentoring you've done with our programme, what kinds of things have you noticed?

"Two things: the first is that at times the female cohort can be unkind to themselves. Within one school, among the female teaching staff there was some nastiness going on behind the scenes, specifically backbiting among female teachers in a dominantly female environment. The simplest solution there was to communicate, which sounds easy but once completed led to a significant relief and better wellbeing across the board for the individual. Interestingly, one of the individuals had no idea how their behaviour was impacting on others.

"The second thing I noticed as a pervading theme was a lack of self-confidence in the individuals coming through the mentoring programme; they did not see themselves as potential leaders, although obviously the senior leadership team of the school did! The rationale in this case is that they joined the teaching profession to teach and by taking a promotion – say, to head of a department – they would be distancing themselves from the thing they loved. So, one of the methods we have discussed is reframing this opportunity as: 'I'm in a new place now. I can standardise teaching across the board in my department.'"

8. Navigating the post-Covid landscape

There was a fence with spaces you
Could look through if you wanted to.
An architect who saw this thing
Stood there one summer evening,
Took out the spaces with great care
And built a castle in the air.
The fence was utterly dumbfounded:
Each post stood there with nothing round it.

Christian Morgenstern

Towards the end of the first Covid-19 lockdown, there was a helpful discussion on the radio between a group of scientists who had been assembled to consider the decisions facing Cobra, the government's cross-departmental Civil Contingencies Committee that convenes to respond to emergencies.

One of the points made was that we should expect to live with the virus for the foreseeable future and plan our lives accordingly. Different risks would have to be contemplated, different decisions taken in comparison with those we might have made before the pandemic. With the development of several effective vaccines we are on slightly firmer ground, but the emergence of new variants could mean things remain unpredictable for some time to come.

As westerners, we have been brought up on a diet of predictions and forecasts: "If you do this, then that will follow," with an implicit (sometimes explicit) assurance of infallibility. A business leader or politician who hedged her bets would be branded as uncertain or ineffectual. Read any party manifesto in the run-up to an election and you will see vote-winning promises, rooted in certainty, which never make it to statute or delivery. In the post-Covid landscape, more of us will open our thinking to tools that might initially appear woolly, in that they ask us to contemplate possibility creation in place of predictive certainty.

Many of the coaching and mentoring clients we have worked with over more than 25 years have come to us seeking support in order to improve their day-to-day performance. Some believed that eventual promotion was possible, but it lay down a particular path containing obstacles and risks that they believed would be difficult, if not impossible, to overcome. For others, the way ahead was so strewn with obstacles that it required a psychological street cleaner of gargantuan proportions to clear it. They perceived themselves as well and truly stuck, with little or no hope of any change. Especially for those in their 30s and 40s, the impact on their motivation and performance was massive when they contemplated occupying the same seat in the staffroom for another 20 or 30 years.

We have seen, in earlier chapters, that coaching and mentoring have the power to transform lives and careers, by raising the individual's awareness and encouraging them to consider different paths from those they assumed were mapped out for them. They had little or no ownership of those maps and the pandemic has had the effect of making those maps redundant, because they chart streets and avenues that are no longer accessible, or else fail to account for the new developments springing up in previously open space. New, untrodden routes and desire lines emerge as quickly as the old ones vanish. Clearly, a new cartography is needed.

The need to understand and adjust to these new surroundings, and to equip oneself with a refined set of skills, can provide the impetus to transform a career. A tool that can reinforce this approach and give it additional grounding is scenario planning. More common in organisations than for individual careers, when applied positively and thoughtfully, perhaps in conjunction with a coaching programme, scenario planning enables the individual to navigate their way through events, even those over which they have scant control.

What have you learned about yourself during the pandemic? What new skills have you acquired, beyond the demands of a Zoom conference? If you have to play a bigger part of your life online, socially and professionally, how will you respond to this proactively?

Scenarios build on the ownership a coachee has gained and translate this ownership into a series of decisions and actions. They broaden the range of alternatives from the single, predictable, dogmatic "official future" into a flexible and dynamic structure of alternative possibilities. The best-laid scenarios include waymarkers, which provide clues as to which of the possible paths that could have been taken actually has been, so as to create and build confidence in the reality we face on a day-to-day basis. For example, if part of a job-seeking scenario includes an interim goal within 12 months to reach the final day of a selection panel, achieving this within six months might suggest both that this is a plausible route to follow and one in which success might be attained earlier than anticipated.

One of the principal benefits of coaching is to raise the awareness of the coachee. We have seen that this is achieved through effective and intelligent questioning from the coach. Initially, this will help to answer questions such as "Do I believe in myself enough to apply for that next job?", "What skills do I need to acquire to be more effective in my current job?" and so on. But if the coachee is part of a school, or other organisation, there is a more macro issue to consider – namely, what is the organisation's awareness? It's not much good the individual being highly aware if the organisation has its head in the sand. That would suggest it's time to move on, or else acquire a large digger.

It was all too apparent in 2020 that most organisations were struggling to navigate their way through the confusing fog of decisions they faced. How can organisational awareness be achieved? If coaching is the means by which an individual raises their awareness, scenario planning does the equivalent job for an organisation.

The most enlightened schools will operate with a planning framework that attempts to envisage the next 3-5 years, in terms of the resources it needs to deploy to achieve its objectives, the tactics it needs to adopt on a day-to-day basis, and perhaps some measure of contingency planning for a rainy day. For all but a minority, this will look like a straight-line extrapolation of their recent past.

It doesn't take an incident as significant as a pandemic to throw such plans off course. More prosaic challenges – such as an outbreak of food poisoning in the school canteen, a staff member using social media inappropriately or a litigious parent – can derail such one-dimensional plans.

Scenario planning raises organisational awareness by getting the school to consider not its predictions of what *will* happen, but instead to consider the possibilities of what *might* take place. Coming into the Covid-19 lockdown, schools would have been armed with plans conceived at a time of relative stability. There would probably have been contingencies for cutting costs, depending on how generous or otherwise they anticipated funding would be, but no provisions for hiring, say, a chief medical officer to reassure parents as to the safety of their children.

In this context, the maps they were using to navigate their route were as much use as those the European explorers used when setting out in search of the New World.

The executive coach Jo Beckett, Bright Field mentee Nick Dennis and I recently got together to see if we could create a framework for education over the next five years. We began by considering which driving forces would impact on the sector in that timeframe. Included among these were issues that might be pertinent in any event, such as regulatory support and endorsement. We thought regulators would also need to consider the impact of the pandemic on their own operations, so they might become less certain or dogmatic in the way they operate.

Other issues emerged that might not have seemed as relevant pre-Covid. We felt one of these, which was both important and less controllable from a school's point of view, was a change in people's interpretation of Maslow's hierarchy of needs. Seen in a positive light, this might mean that there would be greater self-fulfilment. However, a consequence of the pandemic for some might be financial difficulty, cutting back on even basic needs, or worse.

By imagining a series of alternative futures – some more threatening, some highly positive – a school provides a stronger backdrop against which to rehearse and stress-test its responses. Without such preparation, when a school encounters something it hasn't anticipated, its response is improvised at best and may take the organisation closer to the precipice than the original crisis. On the other hand, if the crisis has been anticipated and a plan put in place to cover the eventuality, the risks involved are much lower and, relative to its competition, the school should find itself at a strategic advantage.

One of the key elements of scenario building is to be clear about the school's starting point. This determines the course it needs to steer to achieve its desired outcome. Two years down the line, the world will have shifted, and if the school has created some sensible lead indicators, they will serve as radar that informs the revised course.

Four scenarios for education

Figure 2

Figure 2 sets out the two axes that emerged as a result of the discussions between Jo, Nick and me: they contain the most important and least controllable variables. Less important and more controllable dimensions are subsumed in each of the four possible futures, or worlds.

We took as our time horizon a period five years hence, and the narrative that follows paints a series of possible futures. If we look back from the future to the present day, it is possible to trace a path from our current predicament. The strategic decisions we take in those five years will lead to one or other of these worlds. These are not predictive outcomes – they are built in order to inform our learning about what might happen.

When undertaking this analysis, it is also important to be clear about the school's starting point. The direction of travel will need to be quite different if the school is assumed to be starting at the centre of the axes, rather than from a marooned position in, say, The Road to Nowhere.

1. **I Can't Get No Satisfaction.** In this world, there is greater self-fulfilment at both an individual and organisational level, but we are having to work with the constraint of a regulatory environment that is still determining its post-Covid raison d'être. In this setting, both schools and regulators are frustrated, and this tension in some cases will escalate to a point where there is a standoff between the parties. Those schools that develop strategies to work more harmoniously with inspectors will find themselves moving to Brave New World; others may find themselves closed permanently or encouraged to merge with other providers, perhaps approved or chosen by the regulator.

2. **The Road to Nowhere.** This is the worst of all worlds, with abject poverty, famine and ill health dominating a bleak landscape, compounded by regulatory fragmentation and poor discipline. The only ways to emerge from this scenario are either an alliance with a school enjoying a stronger regulatory relationship, or a sustained campaign to eradicate poverty, poor mental health and the other consequences of this world.

3. **Two Nations.** In contrast to The Road to Nowhere, schools here have the satisfaction of knowing that the regulator is on their side, perhaps as a result of a successful programme of health awareness

led by their new chief medical officer (all schools must appoint one). Their students are learning how to eat more nutritiously, and Ofsted's new health inspection regime has evolved from conversations and meetings between the leading thinkers in schools and recently hired medical inspectors (perhaps graduates of those schools).

4. **Brave New World.** In this world, which might be subtitled Silver Lining, schools and regulators have a positive co-existence. That is not to say that they have reverted to the status quo; that scenario was ruled out globally in the second and third waves of Covid-19. There are strong relationships between schools and their communities, with job-creation programmes sponsored by local firms among the vocational offerings available in the most enlightened schools.

We can imagine our scenarios as a series of acts in a film. When the first phase of our mentoring programme got underway, there were some mentees with significant roles in their senior leadership teams: some assistant heads, some deputies. Not all of them had aspirations to play the starring role of headteacher and it was the tap on the shoulder from their head, who perhaps sensed their potential more clearly, that propelled them on to the programme.

Others might have felt themselves to be, if not extras on a film set, then playing small speaking parts. A savvy director might have seen their ability to play more a significant role, above the title, in perhaps two or three films' time.

At the other end of the career spectrum, a healthy number of heads would have seen a further five to 10 years of leadership as within their compass. They might have assumed that their best years were still ahead of them, when they would be able to consolidate their expertise and perhaps attain a CEO role in a multi-academy trust. Instead, the pandemic will have appeared to many from this cohort as the signal to "spend more time with the family". Although this will pave the way for a younger generation to succeed them, the sector will find itself prematurely robbed of considerable talent.

To conclude this chapter, here are three elements that schools should incorporate into their long-term plans:

1. **Model, support and encourage healthy work-life balance.** Develop a "family first" workplace culture and provide as much flexibility as possible for staff to manage their own lives and support their families/friends at all stages of life.

2. **Engage women in the financial operations of the school.** Provide financial literacy training in basic investment and accounting practices to the entire faculty/staff. Dedicate faculty meetings to review enrolment financials or retirement and pension planning. Involve women in strategic budget planning and delegate areas of management responsibilities to allow them to hone skills.

3. **Resist perfectionism and encourage healthy risk.** Create a school and workplace environment where perfection is not coveted as much as innovation, iteration and learning. Encourage staff to move outside their comfort zone by taking on a new project or responsibility that is beyond their current area of expertise.

9. A different kind of magic: Stephanie McClean on creative expressive workshops

Womanhood and leadership have always been important factors in my life. As for many women of my generation and those before me, these concepts have not necessarily been easy bedfellows. And yet, as a child of the early 1980s, I grew up with the increasing narrative of glass ceilings being shattered and women forging forward into the world of leadership. Now, as an adult, I fully embrace my feminist identity. However, we are in no way "there" yet. With the gender pay gap and a lack of inclusion for women of colour, women with disabilities, and trans and non-binary people, to name but a few issues, we still have a long way to go. My engagement with the mentoring project has its foundations in women's empowerment and particularly the empowerment of women leaders in education, in the hope that they in turn will inspire and help create women leaders of the future in their students.

I first became aware of the project through working with Hilary and Ian, and connecting the work they do with the Insights psychometric with the way I work as a creative arts psychotherapist specialising in dramatherapy. Much of the psychological underpinning of the Insights model (see chapter 10) is based on the Jungian theory of "archetypes", a cast of characters or roles that are innate to our personality and self and whom we engage with throughout our life, which is one of the dominant approaches used by dramatherapists.

As a dramatherapist, I was interested in how, by using dramatherapy techniques such as role play, games, and work with the body and music, there was room for further exploration of what people were discovering about themselves through Insights. Dramatherapy is a form of psychotherapy found in a wide variety of settings, from NHS mental health services to schools and prisons. However, as dramatherapists, we are able to develop and facilitate non-clinical "creative expressive" workshops that are not therapy, but a space where participants are able to explore, play and engage on a creative and expressive level.

Ian invited me and my fellow dramatherapist Kim Hardie to develop and deliver a workshop for the project's first conference at Sandhurst in 2018. As the conference theme was "leadership and identity", it seemed there was a need for a space for delegates to explore, discuss, play and consider who they were as leaders and what leadership meant to them. Due to our varied experiences of group work and professional training, Kim and I were both aware of how valuable a space such as this workshop could be for people, particularly as future leaders.

This idea has been reflected by others:

> *"...for individuals to benefit from processes of leader and leadership development, the conditions of safe spaces must be provided. Spatial boundaries, such as those around leadership development programs in which managers can explore in play (scenarios, simulations, role-plays, outdoor experiences, games and other sorts of play) can encourage departures from existing norms and procedures by allowing people to suspend requirements for consistency and rationality, and, as they play with possibilities, develop new skills or self-images that can be transferred back to their day-to-day work environment."* (Kark, p.512)

The workshop we developed aimed to help the delegates think further about the "archetypes" held within their Insights profile. They chose cards with descriptions of individual archetypes and associated images where they felt an affinity in light of the discoveries they had made through Insights. They were invited to transform their sense of what this archetype meant to them, as a leader, into a physical "statue" they embodied. The group was then split in two and we transformed the space into an imaginary gallery called The Hall of Leaders. Each delegate in one half of the group held their "statue" pose as music played; the other half of the group observed them within the "gallery". Once out of the imaginary gallery, they were able to discuss, share and reflect what that experience was like.

Drawing on many psychological theories, we provided a space where delegates could physically "step into" their potential selves as leaders and be conscious of being witnessed by their peers. This was challenging by design, as it incorporated many different skills utilised by those in leadership positions, such as group collaboration, creative thinking, decision-making, risk-taking, performance, and the acknowledgement of the difference between how we present ourselves physically to others and how we see ourselves internally. We wanted to "make it possible for leaders not yet on the job to realistically anticipate and practice for leadership situations in which they will soon be immersed" (Lippitt, p.287).

We wanted to give colleagues the opportunity to experience a space where they could voice how they felt about embarking on something that was very different from what they may have experienced before. By creating room for discussion, exploration and reflection in a group, they would be able to focus on their personal growth as individuals and how certain situations made them feel. This is such a rare occurrence for people within their professional lives, and yet, given the opportunity to voice emotions in a safe space, many find it hugely valuable and fundamental to recognising that leaders come in many forms.

> *"Leadership development programs that focus on personal growth are reported to have a strong effect on individuals, because much of the work is done on an emotional level."* (Kark, p.513)

The act of facilitating a process for women to be heard and speak openly about their experience within leadership in education is an important one. It has often been observed "how difficult it has been for women to gain a 'voice' within the dominant discourse on school leadership to speak about gender and its continuing importance in both theory and practice in education." (Reynolds, p.2)

In 2019, for the Godolphin and Latymer conference, I chose to develop a slightly different workshop. The theme of the second conference, "challenging assumptions", led me to think about what assumptions might warrant exploration within this area. I asked Hilary to develop the workshop with me, as I wanted input from someone with experience as an educator, an understanding of the challenges of being a woman leader within an education setting, and a good understanding of drama. As a former drama teacher and an experienced coach, Hilary was able to collaborate with me to create a workshop that built on many of the previous concepts Kim and I had used, but had a slightly different focus. Hilary and I wanted to help the delegates think about a variety of aspects of leadership, challenging the assumption that people have to conform to a narrow stereotype of "the leader".

The delegates were asked to work in small groups to discuss and write down the assumptions they had about leadership, identifying one aspect as a theme for their group. They were then asked to choose one person, who was able to physically demonstrate this aspect of leadership, to embody their "leader". They developed their "leader" into more of a character by choosing a name and age; they were then given a scenario for this leader to respond to. Once they had decided how their leader would behave within this scenario, they created a still montage around this character, considering the use of space and the positioning of the rest of the group. Within the rest of the group they developed three distinct roles: the narrator, who described the situation and who the leader was; the outward voice of the leader, who was able to provide statements about what the leader might say to those around them; and the inward voice of the leader, who was able to express their internal narrative. They interpreted these roles and developed them within the scenario, then performed to the other small groups and reflected on the process.

This workshop was designed not only to challenge different aspects of leadership, but also to explore how we function as people within our professional roles. By using a technique taken from the dramatic theorist Augusto Boal, we were able to help the group bring roles and interpersonal dynamics "to life", and project their assumptions, feelings, thoughts and ideas on to the scenarios, as well as their character and roles within them. This projective way of working is often used within creative expressive workshops, allowing people to work freely with aspects of familiar material without it being personal to them.

The experiential aspect of this workshop also provided the delegates with the opportunity to consider what role they chose to take within a group process, to "examine broad aspects such as what each individual does to cope with the anxiety inherent in the group. Does he pair off with another, join a larger group or isolate himself … [we] can look at the roles he exhibits, eg. dominant or passive, leader or led" (Shuttleworth, p.2).

Using a technique by Boal was a deliberate acknowledgement of the ideas behind the use of theatrical techniques to elicit individual and social change. After all, we are considering leadership from a woman's perspective, and to ignore the multifaceted aspects of the challenge innate to women's journeys as leaders would be to deny the echoes of wider psychological, social and cultural implications within this process. Boal used theatre (often via acting and witnessing) as a vehicle for people to examine themselves within their lives, roles and society.

> *"Humans are capable of seeing themselves in the act of seeing, of thinking their emotions, of being moved by their thoughts. They can see themselves here and imagine themselves there; they can see themselves today and imagine themselves tomorrow."* (Boal, p.xxvi)

This process therefore empowers delegates to think about how they are within their professional and personal lives; to consider who they are as people and what leadership means to them. We decided to only provide two different scenarios to the four small groups, meaning that two groups would use the each scenario. This highlighted aspects of difference and similarity: the delegates could compare and contrast different roles within leadership, personality types, group dynamics and discuss their thoughts openly.

> *"The ability to play in a safe environment or time-bounded space can help people develop as leaders. This is because a safe environment enables them to experiment with a range of provisional leadership images, switching from one to the other and adopting various possible selves before settling on a new direction and making transformations in the way they chose to think and act as leaders."* (Kark, p.513)

After developing and facilitating both these workshops, I have been struck by how much more there is to explore. I am aware of the possibility to explore gender further within the dynamics that are already present within these workshops; to open a dialogue around how women fit into the common narrative of leadership and their performative roles within that, in order to form an understanding of what it means to be a woman leader.

> *"...while women themselves have often eschewed the term 'leadership', the ways in which women have undertaken roles and activities that required leadership – however loosely defined – invite an analysis of the term that goes beyond the traditional and conventional masculine understandings of leadership."* (Damousi and Tomsic, p.332)

My involvement in this project has not been about teaching people something they don't already know, or providing mass-marketed "off the shelf" solutions to practical issues within leadership. My interventions have been based on my experience as a psychotherapist, to facilitate a creative process through which people develop their autonomy and awareness to decide how they use the internal resources they already possess in order to navigate the challenges they face.

Recognition of the individual is as valuable in leadership development as it is in any other area of life. Building on a person's sense of their own identity, inherent skill and experience is conducive to building confidence and authentic leadership, which are the foundations of continuous professional and personal development. We don't arrive in a place of responsibility as fully rounded "leaders". We grow into our roles as people and inhabit them in our own way, and move forward in order to empower others to do the same.

> *"For me, becoming isn't about arriving somewhere or achieving a certain aim. I see it instead as forward motion, a means of evolving, a way to reach continuously toward a better self. The journey doesn't end."* (Obama, p.419)

References

Boal, Augusto. (1992) *Games for Actors and Non-Actors*, Routledge

Damousi, Joy, and Tomsic, Mary. (2014) "Conclusion: gender and leadership" in Damousi, Joy, Rubenstein, Kim, and Tomsic, Mary (eds), *Diversity in Leadership: Australian women, past and present*, ANU Press

Kark, Ronit. (2011) "Games managers play: play as a form of leadership development", *Academy of Management Learning & Education*, 10:3, pp.507–527

Lippitt, Ronald. (1943) "The psychodrama in leadership training", *Sociometry*, 6:3, pp.287–292

Obama, Michelle. (2018) *Becoming*, Penguin

Reynolds, Cecilia. (2002) "Introduction: new questions about women and school leadership" in Reynolds, Cecilia (ed), *Women and School Leadership: international perspectives*, State University of New York Press

Shuttleworth, Roy E. (1977) "Dramatherapy in a professional training group", *Dramatherapy*, 1:1, pp.1–7

10. The life-changing potential of psychometrics

Until you make the unconscious conscious, it will direct your life and you will call it fate

Carl Jung

The positive impact of psychometric profiling on mentees has been referred to at several points in this book. The aim of this chapter is to explore the discipline of profiling and feedback, particularly for those who have not been exposed to it and may be curious about its benefits.

My first experience of being profiled was during an interview with Shell in my final year at university. The so-called milkround, when companies and other organisations visited universities seeking to recruit graduates, was very different then from what it is now. As an economics student, I had focused most of my applications on the finance sector and gained second interviews with four of the main banks. I'd also applied to Shell, as its graduate training programme was one of the best regarded, and went on to attend a second interview in London.

The candidates hadn't been told in detail about the psychometric testing process, but after our individual interviews a group of us were asked to assemble in a basement room usually reserved for blood donation. Answering the 16 Personality Factors (16PF) questionnaire had a dizzying effect similar to that experienced when giving blood. No results were made available to the candidates. In the end, I just missed out on the job.

The various questionnaires I have taken over the course of my career fall into three categories. The first I would describe as quizzes of limited worth and poor psychometric quality. They are used by recruiters and others when seeking to determine one's suitability for a particular role. I had to take one of these quizzes when applying for a strategic planning job in a well-known public sector business. One of the dimensions of the questionnaire was ambition. I scored quite low on this quality, and my motivation and ambition were questioned by the recruiter (bear in mind that I was aged the wrong side of 50). I suggested that, having achieved my major career goals some years earlier, my focus now was on using my experience to do a good job for a period of time and then move on. This was clearly not the answer she was expecting, although our argument didn't keep me from being shortlisted.

The second category is characterised by a lack of opportunity to do anything with the results of the questionnaire. During my last four years at Barclays, I was based in a newly created business, the markets division of the investment arm Barclays de Zoete Wedd. Our newly appointed HR director subjected us to a variety of psychometric tools. The most instructive of these were the Herrmann Brain Dominance Instrument and the Margerison-McCann Team Management Profile. Both of these were highly informative and thought-provoking, and the results were ably and professionally fed back to me. The only dilemma I faced was how I could bring about any meaningful change in my career as a consequence.

The third category is characterised by a strong psychometric *and* the opportunity to do something as a consequence. I believe this is the category occupied by the psychometric we use on the mentoring programme, Insights Discovery.

The following case studies illustrate how two of our Bright Field clients – one over a period of time, the other more quickly – were aided by psychometric profiling to take opportunities in quite different settings.

Case study: Louise H

Occasionally, the power of psychometric feedback can, literally, be life-changing. Some years ago, I was working with the marketing department of a financial services company. My client had singled out a colleague whom he valued highly, but whose day-to-day performance needed reinforcing. When we met for the first time, Louise was delighted to have been chosen for this work. Helpfully, she had been reassured by her boss that there was nothing remedial in the intervention we were discussing – it was very much about helping her to raise her game still further.

After an initial conversation, Louise took one of the psychometric questionnaires we use before initiating a coaching dialogue. The creative energy I had detected in our first meeting shone out in the results and in her profile. When I presented the results to Louise, it was as though a weight had been lifted from her shoulders – one that, it transpired, had its origins in her childhood.

"I always told my mother I was artistic," she said. "I had wanted to do art at A-level, but was put off by my parents telling me I would struggle to get a decent job with that qualification. This [she pointed to the highest-scoring element of the graph] proves what I thought: I *am* creative, yet this job doesn't tap any of that aspect of my personality. I'm going to ring my mother tonight and tell her about this. You've changed my life!"

Reflecting on the conversation recently, Louise said: "What makes your intervention even more life-changing is the fact that I was shoehorned into operational delivery roles rather than the creative marketing roles. Your coaching was my springboard into business development roles, where creativity was key to identifying unique opportunities for the company to work with other large companies, where at first glance there appeared to be no mutual commercial opportunity.

"You helped me make sense of myself, really know myself, and eradicated the self-doubt instilled by certain colleagues. I changed my environment, was able to eventually obtain redundancy, and began a new career far removed from the marketing of financial services. I couldn't be happier."

Case study: Rachel M

I had been coaching Chris, a PhD student coming to the end of nearly seven years at the same university, when he mentioned that his partner was in a similar position. Chris had finally acknowledged that he had to decide what job he should consider – something he had been putting off for years. His partner, Rachel, had been at university for six years so far, and had a year until she was due to complete her doctoral thesis. But she had already decided that she was ready to start exploring her options.

This was during the first Covid-19 lockdown, and I had briefly met Rachel during one of my Zoom calls with Chris. Now, for our first one-on-one call, I took Rachel through the results of her Insights profile. She was already familiar with the model, having read Chris's report a few weeks earlier, and was pleased and surprised to see how accurate her own report was.

She described the work she had been doing for her thesis, which concerned skin treatments and creams used to alleviate moisture-associated skin damage. She had decided that, despite her success with the research she had carried out, she did not wish to continue with that work once she had graduated. She was looking for something different, but was not sure what that might look like.

It also became apparent that she was keen to explore how to be more robust in the face of criticism from professional colleagues. Some of this related to her thesis research, but, more worryingly, she was being subjected to gender bias from the predominantly male fellow researchers.

In our second session, we started to explore Rachel's different options. Using a decision-making tool linked to the psychometric, Rachel listed her initial options. They felt like possibilities she had already discounted, and there was little or no energy in her voice or body language when she described them.

I asked her whether there were any other ideas she might have had but not considered recently. It appeared there was something – and Rachel began to speak in a much more animated way. She said part of her research concerned how skin reacts to medical treatment, and explained that a large proportion of people of all ages suffering from incontinence also have to deal with the side effect of incontinence-associated dermatitis.

"The creams can be expensive and they differ greatly in their properties," Rachel said. "Better treatments might exist for people, but they aren't well-advertised to consumers. Also, different NHS trusts prescribe differently, so not all appropriate treatments are available, despite the fact that they might work better. People often stick to what they know, rather than experimenting to find the best treatment. Part of this is due to cost and another factor is the lack of guidance in the area and the stigma of incontinence, meaning people are less likely to seek help.

"Not all of the treatments are available on the NHS, but if the patient finds them off-putting, they are deterred from trying something else by the cost involved and by the waste of the current medication – none of the products are available in small sizes.

"Maternity units in hospitals make what are called Bounty Bags available to new mothers, which contain nappies, creams and related products, enabling the parents to try their preferred products before committing to them. I think something similar would be helpful for older patients." Rachel's idea was to make sample boxes of different medications available to patients, so they could try out the options before committing to the one they preferred.

I fed back to Rachel that the energy she was using to describe this possibility was very different from her mood earlier in the call. Had she talked about the idea to anyone? "I mentioned it to Chris the other day when we were talking about my profile, but apart from that I haven't taken it any further."

I asked Rachel to give it some further thought before our next session, to see if she could come up with a possible name for the idea and to describe what the simplest version of the product would look like. In a previous role, I had worked with a new product development process, and this was one of early exercises we had used with our clients in those days. One had been a leading retail pharmaceutical company and I put Rachel in touch with a member of that team. I also gave her the name of another former colleague in a leading pharmaceutical firm.

A month later, Rachel was keen to tell me about the progress she had made. "I spoke to Tim and he suggested that I consider a couple of options, one of which I really like the sound of. We also explored the differences between different people and cultures, which can influence product preferences.

"The current pandemic is affecting a number of businesses in the healthcare and cosmetics business, and they are keen to see how they can reach new customers with their samples. As well as the idea I have for incontinence products, I think one thing we could offer is a sampling service for things like speciality soaps, balms and related products. That would also allow us to see how viable our packing and delivery model is."

Rachel had also identified a gap in the market for product samples that were not packaged in plastic. "Plastic sachets are hugely wasteful and consumers are demanding more eco-friendly products. When it comes to the medical treatment boxes, this may not be possible to achieve as many products do come in plastic tubes and pots – this is highly sanitary and I think, in some areas, a balance is required. Where we can be plastic-free, let's all try our best, but in the instance of medical supplies – e.g. PPE and medical products – the need is there to continue using these products until manufacturing processes and pharmaceutical companies adapt."

Reflecting at later date, Rachel noted that, before our first meeting, "I was keen to get out of the toxic environment, but was nervous about the decision-making process that would enable me to get a fulfilling career. My biggest challenge was that I had lost confidence in myself and saw too many obstacles in navigating the way to a fulfilling career.

"The most impactful part of the first session was running through the decision matrix for career options. The first time I filled it in, I played it safe with my career-option choices. I then reread the template and realised that I hadn't entered any of my dreams at all; instead I had written the paths I thought I should take based on my academic background. I then redid the sheet with responses that were more aligned with my dreams and ambitions. The fact that you showed positivity, enthusiasm and genuine interest was enlightening and enabled me to come out of my shell, and to not block and shy away from my aspirations.

"I felt empowered and ready to begin my own start-up company. At the start, this was only a dream which I had pretty much dismissed, but now I have formed the company and I'm on the journey to make it into something special."

A few weeks later there was a knock at my front door. It was a courier carrying a cardboard box branded with the logo "Sample and Shop". Inside was a collection of men's toiletries in sample-sized containers, the first fruits of Rachel's new business.

Conclusion

Omnia Feminae Aequissimae (women are equal to everything)

**Motto of Lady Hale,
first female president of the Supreme Court**

Among the women it's been our privilege to meet during the years of planning and delivering the mentoring programme, Lady Hale stands out for her achievements, clarity and steadfastness. I first met her at the 2018 Association of State Girls' Schools conference, where she was a keynote speaker. In 2019, she rose to national prominence after the Supreme Court's verdict that the government acted unlawfully in its decision to prorogue Parliament.

Lady Hale also spoke at the 2019 ASGS conference, attracting headlines for her apparent reference to Boris Johnson's use of the phrase "girly swot". She said that, at Cambridge, "I was a girly swot and there were quite a few young men who were, similarly, girly swots – they wanted to get on with their work and their lives."

If there is a theme to this book, it is summed up by Lady Hale's motto, *Omnia Feminae Aequissimae*. Of course, the lessons in this book relate to women working in all types of schools. But at a time when the continued existence of many girls' schools is in doubt, and when others are deciding to go coed, we wanted to use this opportunity to highlight some key strategic decisions that the girls' school sector in particular could usefully adopt.

Everything changes

Many of the schools we have worked with do not have an explicit policy of professional development, aimed at future leaders, which would reinforce the message of Lady Hale's motto. There seems to be an expectation that girls will aspire to be at least the equal of men in their chosen careers, without more than token examples of women's leadership in the ranks of the staff. The Covid-19 pandemic is likely to exacerbate this trend, even if most schools have developed approaches to maintain or enhance staff resilience in the face of unhelpful and contradictory government policies.

In Chapter 8, the scenarios for alternative futures highlighted the significance of greater self-actualisation in the post-pandemic world. Whenever what economists refer to as a "discontinuity" occurs – brought about, for example, by war, recession or pandemic – those organisations that were the sector leaders before the discontinuity are rarely the leaders after it. The rules change; the criteria required for success change. Unless schools recognise that a new paradigm is necessary, characterised by more teacher-supportive strategies than hitherto, they will find themselves on The Road to Nowhere.

Our former colleague Steve Glowinkowski helpfully distinguishes between the climate of an organisation and its culture. Climate is defined as "what it feels like to work here", whereas culture is "how things are done here". Each is measurable. In his book *It's Behaviour, Stupid!*, Glowinkowski writes: "All things being equal, Climate differentiates an average from an outstandingly performing organisation ... Whatever the level of performance currently being achieved by an organisation, an improvement in its Climate will improve its performance measured across a range of bottom-line outcomes ... a measurable, positive shift in leadership behaviours will drive a quantifiable improvement in the Climate."

We recommend, therefore, that schools should devote more time and resources to the development of leadership capabilities in their outstanding staff. Chris Wright, when education director at Woodard Schools, was impressed by the amount of time that leading commercial organisations devote to professional development in order to maintain and enhance their own pipelines of staff development. The OECD's annual *Education at a Glance* report has identified the high proportion of time that teachers in England spend in front of a class. In comparison with most other developed countries, much less time is given over to preparation and pastoral support.

There is an undeniable business case for schools to create more time for leadership development. Rather than hiring new blood to fill headteacher, bursar and senior staff vacancies, via the services of recruiters or headhunters, schools that grow their own talent bases could likely save themselves a reasonable amount of money, with benefits to both performance and morale. Recruiters have their place, but when used merely to confirm a governing body's hunch they do not add value. Too often, selection committees are looking for headteacher candidates who already have headteacher experience, but this fails to nurture, recognise and reward the leadership potential that already exists within the school.

There is a need across the sector for more system leaders – those heads who see their responsibility beyond the school gates and work actively, perhaps as national leaders of education, to promote best practice. In a number of schools, we have come across examples of colleagues whose leadership potential has not been developed or encouraged by their headteacher. Fear of losing good leaders to rival schools, and concerns that procuring replacement staff would be time-consuming and expensive, lie at the heart of such short-termism.

The lessons provided by the Army are also worth highlighting. We have heard in this book how Lucy Giles and Amanda Hassell have evolved formal and informal processes for identifying talent. Once spotted, increasingly structured training and development processes are put in place so that when an individual's next post is agreed, they have a much greater level of preparation and a much greater chance of being successful in that role than someone parachuted in at short notice.

Leadership development does not need to be an expensive process. The vast majority of the schools we work with have governing bodies and trustees with considerable leadership talent. Those talents could be brought to bear in a mentoring programme similar in design to the one we have evolved. And we have seen in this book just how powerful the one-to-one relationship between mentee and mentor can be. The intimacy of being listened to; the space and time to explore and discuss; the opportunity to put themselves first for a change – it is these aspects of mentoring that have helped mentees on our programme to, in the words of St Thomas, "bring forth what is within you".

Anyone can be a leader

As Caroline Hoare, Floyd Steadman and Gwen Byrom have observed in these pages, governing bodies have to look beyond the status quo when it comes to recruiting leaders. They have to be encouraged to recognise their unconscious biases. When presented with her psychometric profile report, one leading headteacher client asked, "Aren't all heads extrovert thinkers like me?" My reply to her was that there's no one type of leadership – our database of headteacher profiles is testament to that. The need to adapt and connect in order to reach staff, students and stakeholders of different predispositions and backgrounds has become paramount as a consequence not just of the pandemic, but also the Black Lives Matter and Everyone's Invited debates. Leaders don't have to look a certain way. It's not about being alpha, or a ball-breaker. It's about having a vision and bringing people along with you.

This misperception that leaders look and sound and behave in a certain way is a key factor in impostor syndrome. Impostor syndrome is not confined to women, but for those colleagues who experience it, external validation can make a huge difference to their confidence and self-perception. When that validation comes from someone outside education, the impact can be all the more powerful.

When we shared the original design of our mentoring programme, there were some raised eyebrows at the idea of using non-educators as our mentors. There remains a resistance to what is sometimes characterised as the "businessification" of education. It may not be appropriate for a corporate parent to offer their well-intentioned services to a headmistress or her SLT, but objective, independent, skilled mentors bring a powerful and valued external perspective to colleagues considering the next steps in their careers – whether those mentors come from inside or outside education.

The pool of female talent in schools is extraordinary. In responding to the challenge we were set by Caroline Jordan and Sharon Cromie, we have tried, in conjunction with our mentors, to break the glass ceiling and change the climate in those schools we have worked with. And this approach and philosophy are set to reach a wider audience: we have been asked by the National Coalition of Girls' Schools in the US and the Alliance of Girls' Schools Australasia to support them to create a Global Mentoring Network for Aspiring Leaders. There is much more work to be done – and it turns out we are just getting started.

Appendix: list of mentors

Helen Beck, partner, Deloitte

Jo Beckett, independent consultant

Michael Blacker, former chair, Business and Oversight Board, Law Society

Samantha Brook, group HR director, Severfield

Helen Browning, chief executive, Soil Association

Helen Burton, independent consultant

Kate Campbell, systemic psychotherapist and social worker

Rob Clift, independent consultant

Kate Cooper, executive director, Birmingham Food Council

John Cridland, former director-general, Confederation of British Industry

Jane Deal, IT director, Law Society

Trish Dooley, independent consultant

Anne Douglas, Major, British Army

Mike Ellwood, non-executive director

Tim Franklin, chairman, PCF Group

Sally Franks, independent consultant

Lucy Giles, Colonel, British Army, and president, Army Officer Selection Board

Jonathan Gorst, head of regeneration and development, London Borough of Southwark

Amanda Hassell, Colonel, British Army

Jane Held, independent consultant

Caroline Hoare, former chief executive, Independent Schools Inspectorate, and former director of people, Girls' Day School Trust

Anna Howard, independent consultant

Simon Lloyd, non-executive director and former HR director, Santander

Jenny Lloyd-Jenkins, executive coach, Elavon Financial Services

Liz Oliver, independent consultant

Steve Pateman, chief executive, Arora Group

Richard Pelly, non-executive director

Mel Robinson, Commodore Maritime Reserves

Janet Thomas, chief executive, Intellect, and former president, Women in Banking and Finance

Jeremy Tomlinson, independent consultant

Angela Wakelin, chief operating officer, Kroo

Julia Warren, group HR director, Trinity Mirror

Tania Watson, independent consultant

Suzanne White, independent consultant

Hilary Wigston, director, Bright Field Consulting

Lisa Worgan, independent consultant

Margaret Wrightson, independent consultant

Denise Yates, non-executive director and former chief executive, Potential Plus UK

Acknowledgements

David Whitaker is at the top of our list of people to thank. It was David who introduced me (Ian) to the power of coaching more than 30 years ago. Together with Sue Whitaker, David's support, guidance and coaching, whether by phone, Zoom or over the dinner table, has been instrumental in shaping our thinking for this book.

Ian Clarkson was our first chairman and mentor when we established Bright Field. He provided much wisdom and foresight in the early days of the business, and when we debated the merits of a pro bono mentoring programme. Mike Gibbons was an early supporter of our work that preceded this programme. His encouragement and appreciation has been a continuing source of strength.

At Insights, Andy Lothian, Vivien Buchan, Susan Stewart, Elaine MacDonald, Debbie Skrobot and Lynne McLagan, in their different and valuable ways, have been a source of continuing support and inspiration in enabling their profiling and other tools to be used in the vital work of education.

Three outstanding educators alerted us to the possibilities of mentoring in girls' schools: Charlotte Avery, Caroline Jordan and Sharon Cromie. They passed the baton helpfully to Frances Ramsey and then Nicky Bright (Botterill) at the Girls' Schools Association, where Jane Carroll has been a continuing and thoughtful presence since the inception of the programme.

Our mentors are an impressive group of individuals and have each enjoyed highly successful careers in the public sector, military or the commercial world. They were willing to give freely of their time and the achievements of their mentees are a testament to their questioning, listening and mentoring skills.

Headteachers in some of the country's best known and highest achieving schools were willing to entrust their brightest and most talented staff to a fledgling programme. My thanks to Anita Bath, Caroline Braggs, Jenny Brown, Gwen Byrom, Jackie Cahalin, Carole Cameron, Kevin Carson, Carol Chandler-Thompson, Sarah Creasey, Natasha Dangerfield, Meryl Davies, Desmond Deehan, Jo Duncan, Julian Dutnall, Jenny Dwyer, Neil Enright, Evelyn Forde, Marina Gardiner Legge, Melissa George, Kathryn Gorman, Denise Gould, Bronwen Goulding, Heather Hanbury, Liz Hewer, Anne Hudson, Lindsey Hughes, Alison Jerrard, Tracy Johnson, Ros Kamaryc, Julie Keller, Anna King, Felicia Kirk, Tracy Kirnig, Sarah Labram, Liz Laybourn, Jane Lunnon, Catherine May, Emma McKendrick, Jessica Miles, Linda Moule, Simone Niblock, Jo Pomeroy, Rae Potter, Sarah Raffray, Lynne Renwick, Judy Rowe, Matthew Shoults, Nicola Smillie, Christine Smith, Rachel Smith, Ricki Smith, Jo Storey, Bex Tear, Elizabeth Thomas, Richard Tillett, Amber Waite, Nicola Walters, Rachael Warwick, Julia Waters, Amy Whitall, Alex Wilson and Katharine Woodcock.

Nearly 100 colleagues have been mentored over the first three cohorts of the programme. Our thanks are due to all of them for entrusting us with their challenges and triumphs, before and during the pandemic.

I realised early in the process of writing this book that I was going to need some creative support. Two talented authors helped a novice writer translate raw ideas into hard and hopefully readable copy: Hannah Copley and Derek Niemann.

At John Catt, Alex Sharratt and Jonathan Barnes believed in and supported the premise of the book. The wonderful Isla McMillan brought her awareness of the education world to bear with her shrewd and supportive editing.

For our conferences at Sandhurst and Godolphin and Latymer, our dramatherapists Steph McClean and Kim Hardie devised outstanding workshops that challenged and stimulated the participants. Together with our keynote speakers – David Laws, Helen Browning, Susan Ferrier,

Juliet Stevenson, Commodore Mel Robinson, Kim Jarred and Mike Murphy – they provided examples of leadership and decision-making that spanned the military, theatre, politics, commerce and agriculture. Henrie Hall provided priceless front-of-house help at short notice. Steve Wilkinson, a friend for more than 50 years, directed a team of film-makers and photographers to give us a wonderful archive of material for the current cohort of mentees and future generations. Ben Denison and Duncan Kitchin reinforced the key moments of the conferences with their photographic skills.

Our thanks are also due to John Gilbert, Nancy McJunkin and Jeff Droker, who live at the opposite ends of the world, yet have shared their wisdom and kindness unstintingly over many years. Trudy Hall's odyssey in Somaliland will doubtless produce a book of its own in due course and it has been a privilege to share that journey with her.

At the National Coalition of Girls' Schools in the US, Megan Murphy and Jen Evers have witnessed the power of this work and led the development of its next iteration. With Loren Bridge at the Alliance of Girls' Schools Australasia, they have built, in conjunction with the Girls' Schools Association in the UK, a formidable network for the next generation of leaders to explore.

Further reading

Ahmed, Murad. (2016) "Is Myers-Briggs up to the job?", *FT Magazine*

The Army Leadership Code: an introductory guide (2015)

Autry, James A. (1996) *Confessions of an Accidental Businessman*, Berrett-Koehler

Avery, Gillian. (1991) *The Best Type of Girl: a history of girls' independent schools*, Andre Deutsch

Brearley, Mike. (2017) *On Form*, Little, Brown

Browning, Helen, with Finney, Tim. (2018) *Pig: tales from an organic farm*, Wildfire

Carman, Dominic. (2013) *Heads Up: the challenges facing England's leading head teachers*, Thistle Publishing

Claxton, Guy (2005) *The Wayward Mind: An Intimate History of the Unconscious*, Little, Brown

Collins, Jim. (2001) *Good to Great: why some companies make the leap... and others don't*, Random House

Collins, Jim. (2005) *Good to Great and the Social Sectors*, Random House

Collins, Jim, and Porras, Jerry I. (1999) *Built to Last: successful habits of visionary companies*, Harper Business

Confederation of British Industry. (2012) *First Steps: a new approach for our schools*

Criado Perez, Caroline. (2019) *Invisible Women: exposing data bias in a world designed for men*, Chatto & Windus

Durcan, Jim, and Oates, David. (1993) *The Manager As Coach: developing your team for maximum performance*, Financial Times Management Series

Eberhardt, Jennifer. (2019) *Biased: the new science of race and inequality*, William Heinemann

Evans, Gail. (2001) *Play Like a Man, Win Like a Woman: what men know about success that women need to learn*, Broadway

Flett, Christopher V. (2007) *What Men Don't Tell Women About Business: opening up the heavily guarded alpha male playbook*, John Wiley & Sons

Glowinkowski, Steve. (2009) *It's Behaviour, Stupid! What really drives the performance of your organisation*, Ecademy Press

Hattenstone, Simon. (2020) "Lady Hale: 'My Desert Island Judgments? Number one would probably be the prorogation case'", *The Guardian*

Hillman, James, and Meade, Michael. (1998) *Character and Destiny: authentic threads of life*, Oral Traditions

HM Treasury. (2020) *Magenta Book: central government guidance on Evaluation*

Husain, Mishal. (2018) *The Skills: how to win at work*, Fourth Estate

Jacobi, Jolande. (1973) *The Psychology of CG Jung*, Yale University Press

Jung, CG. (1964) "Approaching the unconscious" in *Man and his Symbols*, Aldus Books

Kets de Vries, Manfred FR. (2021) *The CEO Whisperer: meditations on leadership, life, and change*, Palgrave Macmillan

Kings College London. (2019) "'Every woman who doesn't call herself a feminist has kept her Wonderbra and burnt her brain.' Kathy Lette talks to Julia Gillard"

Kothari, Tina. (2008) *Women in Leadership: five routes to success in business*, Arena Books

Leahy, Maria Marsella, and Shore, Rebecca Ann. (2018) *Journeys of Charter School Creators: leadership for the long haul*, Rowman & Littlefield

Locke, John L. (2011) *Duels and Duets: why men and women talk so differently*, Cambridge University Press

Margolis, Jane, and Fisher, Allan. (2003) *Unlocking the Clubhouse: women in computing*, MIT Press

Marquet, L David. (2012) *Turn the Ship Around! A true story of turning followers into leaders*, Penguin

Nonaka, Ikujiro, and Takeuchi, Hirotaka. (1995) *The Knowledge-Creating Company: how Japanese companies create the dynamics of innovation*, Oxford University Press

Porritt, Vivienne, and Featherstone, Keziah (eds). (2019) *10% Braver: inspiring women to lead education*, Sage Publications

Rippon, Gina. (2019) *The Gendered Brain: the new neuroscience that shatters the myth of the female brain*, Bodley Head

Rivers, Caryl, and Barnett, Rosalind C. (2013) *The New Soft War on Women: how the myth of female ascendance is hurting women, men – and our economy*, Tarcher

Robinson, Ken. (2001) *Out of Our Minds: learning to be creative*, Capstone Publishing

Sandberg, Sheryl. (2013) *Lean In: women, work, and the will to lead*, WH Allen

Schwartz, Peter. (1992) *The Art of the Long View: scenario planning – protecting your company against an uncertain world*, Century Business

Thomson, Peninah, and Laurent, Clare. (2015) *The Rise of the Female Executive: how women's leadership is accelerating cultural change*, Palgrave Macmillan

Turner, Toko-pa. (2017) *Belonging: remembering ourselves home*, Her Own Room Press

Varkey Foundation. (2017) *What the World's Young People Think and Feel: Generation Z – global citizenship survey*

Whitaker, David. (1999) *The Spirit of Teams*, Crowood Press

Whitmore, John. (1992) *Coaching for Performance: a practical guide for growing your own skills*, Nicholas Brealey